RUM

Edible

Series Editor: Andrew F. Smith

EDIBLE is a revolutionary series of books dedicated to food and drink that explores the rich history of cuisine. Each book reveals the global history and culture of one type of food or beverage.

Already published

Rum

A Global History

Richard Foss

REAKTION BOOKS

Published by Reaktion Books Ltd
Unit 32, Waterside
44–48 Wharf Road
London N1 7UX, UK
www.reaktionbooks.co.uk

First published 2012
Reprinted 2016, 2019

Printed and bound in China by 1010 Printing International Ltd

British Library Cataloguing in Publication Data
Foss, Richard
Rum : a global history. – (Edible)
1. Rum – History.
2. Cooking (Rum)
I. Title II. Series
641.2´59´09-DC23

ISBN 978 1 86189 926 2

Contents

Liquid History:
An Introduction

The first time I enjoyed the flavour of rum was not the first time I actually drank it – far from it, in fact. I had imbibed rum as a teenager, of the quality that someone would bring to a party frequented by underage drinkers, and I could not imagine how anyone could enjoy drinking the stuff straight. That particular rum and I both had plenty of rough edges, and we did not immediately take to each other. I drank rum, then and later, as a component of sweet tropical drinks with umbrellas in them, and occasionally as an addition to coffee on cold evenings. My conversion to actively appreciating good rum came as an accident as I sought to win the heart of a fair lady.

The woman was a few years older than me and far more sophisticated, and I was more than a bit nervous on our first date. We arrived early for a dinner reservation and were invited to wait in the bar, and she confidently ordered, 'Myers's and rocks, please.' Having no idea what that was, I added, 'Sounds great! Make that two.' A coffee-coloured liquid with ice cubes arrived in short order, and I cautiously took a sip. It was obviously a distilled spirit of some kind, but like nothing I had tried before: smooth and gentle and tasting delicately of spice and caramel. When my date left for a few moments on

Myers's rum used a simple but memorable graphic style for many ads, as in this example from 1941.

some mysterious feminine errand, I asked the bartender for a look at the bottle so I could find out what this marvellous elixir was.

Rum? *That* was rum?

My romantic intentions with the lady fizzled out shortly thereafter, but my appreciation for her beverage of choice grew with each new experience. I savoured light and dark, sweet and spicy, mellow and sharp. Gradually I learned some of the lore of rum, the extraordinary history and cultural connections that go far beyond the superficial connection with tiki drinks, Caribbean pirates and bad sea shanties.

The most famous of these, the one with the 'Yo, ho, ho, and a bottle of rum' chorus, isn't traditional at all – it was written by Robert Louis Stevenson for his book *Treasure Island* in 1883. This is in keeping with much pirate and rum lore, both of which are full of romantic misinformation. The truth about both rum and piracy is actually more interesting. Rum has been a beverage, a currency and an element of ritual, a symbol of debauchery among Temperance crusaders and of healthy moderation in the British Navy. It is made as far south as New Zealand and as far north as Newfoundland, and was a major export of colonial New England. Rum has jump-started economies and fuelled the slave trade, sparked mutinies against captains who withheld it and governors who tried to regulate it, and been an indispensable element of religious worship. It has been celebrated by authors, used in toasts by statesmen, and also been a comfort and reward to the labourers who cut the cane that went to make more rum. In recent years aged versions have acquired, and deserved, the same mystique as fine Scotch whisky, and a new generation of distillers are creating surprising variants on traditional recipes.

In short, it is a beverage that is every bit as worthy of study as wine, but that hasn't generally attracted the same level of consideration. This brief book alone will not make up for that deficit, but will give at least an overview of rum's origins, worldwide history and cultural impact, and perhaps a glimpse at its future. There are other books about the early history of rum in the Caribbean that go into greater detail, but none that address rum as a worldwide phenomenon. I will also explore some aspects of the anthropology of rum, the songs and poems that celebrated it or attacked it as evil. Rum has provoked strong feelings from the very beginning, and it would be easy to fill a book twice this size with its lore and literature.

I

What Is and Isn't Rum?

First it's worth a look at the question of what rum is, which is not as easy to answer as it might seem. The simplest definition is that rum is a beverage distilled from sugar cane, either in the form of the raw juice or from molasses refined from sugar by boiling. That seems to be an easy line to draw, but in practice things get murky.

Pure sugar-cane juice can be fermented into a type of rum usually called *rhum agricole* or cachaça, and about 10 per cent of the world's rum is made this way. Almost all of this is produced either in Brazil or in former French colonies, though boutique distillers elsewhere are expanding the style. There is no generally accepted generic term for rums based on sugar-cane juice – distillers in the French Caribbean argue that only their products should be called *rhum agricole*, and Brazilian law says that cachaça can only be produced in that country. (It might seem that cachaça is just another word for rum from Brazil, but there are also Brazilian rums that are marketed just as rum. Cachaça is distilled to a lower proof than most other rums, and batches are started with a different technique, but these reasons alone are not enough to consider it something other than a form of rum.)

Throughout this book I will use the term 'cane rum' as a generic for rums made from sugar-cane juice rather

This 1830 engraving of a sugar plant by Sir William Hooker is an example of beautiful scientific art from before the age of photography.

than molasses. Such rums are usually more expensive than molasses-based rums, both because the starting product is more valuable and because of the relatively low efficiency of this type of operation. Cane rum can only be made when the sugar plants are ripe and producing fresh juice, so they are idle for part of the year. Molasses-based rums can be made all year round from stored product.

Distillers who use molasses as a raw material are unlikely to adopt the French term for their rums, which is *rhum industriel*. The distinction seems explicitly designed to make cane rum appear more healthy. (While the French were generally behind in rum technology, their marketing skills were acute.) Molasses is the sludge that is left over from boiled cane juice after the crystalline sugar has been extracted; that which isn't made into rum is usually bottled for culinary uses or added to animal feed. There is a very wide range of flavours in raw molasses, based on the variety of cane, soil and climate. For instance, Brazilian molasses is particularly sweet and light,

Sugar cane juice being cooked into molasses in Racine, West Virginia, in 1903.

while Fijian molasses made by the same process is acrid and approximately twice as dark. In addition, there are several distinctions among the grades of syrup left over from sugar processing. In Britain and former British colonies, the first distilling is called light molasses, the second dark treacle or dark molasses, while the third is called blackstrap molasses. Rum of varying quality can be made from all of these, though liquor made from the lower grades of syrup is usually redistilled to remove pungent flavours.

Any kind of sugar processing will produce molasses as a waste product, but only some kinds are desirable for making rum. Sugar-beet processing creates molasses that can be made into alcohol, but alkaline salts that are concentrated in the process make the resulting rum unpalatable. Maple syrup can be made into rum, but the high price of the raw ingredient compared to cane molasses makes it economically impractical. (Maple trees are only about 5 per cent as productive as sugar cane, and produce sap only for a short season, while sugar cane is productive for most of the year in tropical climates.) Sorghum refining produces molasses that can be used to make rum, and some boutique distillers have experimented with rums based wholly or in part on sorghum, but their marketing efforts have been hampered by the fact that US and EU law require anything that is labelled as rum to be made from sugar-cane products. A few companies in Africa and China make sorghum rum for local consumption, but for cultural reasons most of the rum that is made this way is labelled 'whiskey'. (In Asia the word 'whiskey' is used for any distilled alcohol, and beverages like Thai Mekhong whiskey are made from 95 per cent molasses and 5 per cent rice.) There are also Chinese and Indian 'whiskies' that are actually rums made in whole or in part from molasses, some of which are very good. Low-quality molasses-based spirits from China are often flavoured with ginseng and medicinal herbs and called *chiew*. These are popular in overseas Chinese communities as an aperitif and medicine, but since the rum is just a spirit base for the herb flavourings, *chiew* will not be dealt with in this book.

The situation is even more confusing with beverages called *aguardiente*, which are made in countries from Mexico to Argentina and in scattered former Spanish colonies. Some *aguardientes* are actually rums by another name, some are made from rum flavoured with anise and herbs, while others are distilled from grape spirits and raisin extract in the style of grappa. *Aguardiente* comes from the term *agua ardiente* – literally, firewater – and the term was used throughout the Spanish Empire to refer to any very strong spirit. Some cane-derived *aguardientes* from Colombia and Mexico are sophisticated and smooth, while others would be recognized as raw white lightning by any bootlegger.

(Oddly, though modern distillers have been exploring new frontiers in other regards, almost all distil from cane juice or molasses without mixing the two. I have only found only one company that regularly distils from a blend of cane and molasses: Ron Los Valientes is made near Veracruz, Mexico.)

Just to confuse things further, there have been other beverages that were called rum, but that were not made from sugar or molasses. In the nineteenth century, European distillers in countries that had no sugar-producing colonies created a beverage they called '*inlander* rum'. This was actually a mix of grain alcohols flavoured and coloured to taste like dark rum. Over the years major companies such as Stroh of Austria that used to make inlander rum this way have changed the formula to use imported molasses. Thanks to this change, which was made partly to comply with EU regulations on what can be called rum, all inlander rums now sold legally are the real thing.

Laws concerning truth in labelling and other social changes have put an end to the most flagrant counterfeits of rum, which were sold during the Soviet period when trade with the outside world was limited. Cuban rum was a major trade item in the Eastern Bloc, but ordinary Soviet citizens could only afford domestic inlander-style imitations. Since they had never tasted the real thing, they had no idea that this 'rum' was bogus. Cuban officers who trained at Soviet naval bases on the Black Sea knew differently, and were horrified when they tried the local swill. Having tried a shot of the stuff while at the Kuban Hotel in Varna, Bulgaria, when I visited the country over two decades ago, I can report that it had a strange metallic taste that was not fully masked by the addition of low-grade fruit juice. One of the many benefits to civilization of the collapse of the Soviet Union is the extinction of these liquors.

Among beverages that actually are rum as it is conventionally defined, there is no single standard for grading and grouping, though many have been proposed. Rums are generally characterized as light, gold or dark, though they come in shades ranging from completely clear to inky black. A darker colour is usually, though not always, a sign that the rum has been aged. Most light rums are clear and unaged, but there are exceptions: some aged rums are filtered so that they become clear again. There are also cheap dark rums that are unaged, but have had caramel flavour and colour added to simulate the ageing process.

As with Scotch whisky, most rum distillers favour used barrels that were previously used for wines or bourbon in order to infuse their product with more complex flavours during the ageing process. Ageing times vary: some countries require that rum be cellared a minimum of eight months to be called aged, others require two years, and most have no

legal requirement at all. Even three or four years is far shorter than the minimum ageing times for brandies and Scotch whiskies, but this does not mean that aged rums are less complex. The warm temperatures in the regions where sugar cane thrives mean that alcohols mature in the barrel much more quickly than in cool climates. This is a benefit to distillers who age their rum, though they also lose more to evaporation in the process.

The flavour of rum can be influenced by many factors – the characteristics of the strain of sugar cane, the age at which it is harvested, the purity of the molasses, how many times the molasses is distilled and to what proof, and how the resulting alcohol is aged. This allows vast latitude for an accomplished producer to create different effects, and for at least 400 years distillers and cellarmasters have experimented and honed their skills.

As Much as You Need to Know About Distilling to Keep Reading

Distilling, the process of concentrating essences from a fermented mixture called wort, is usually credited to Arab and Persian alchemists of the Middle Ages. This assumption was overturned when a complete terracotta still was identified in a museum in Taxila, Pakistan, and estimated to be 5,000 years old. It is a simple thing, a dome-lidded clay pot with a detachable spout that empties into a covered bowl, but anyone who has visited a modern distillery can recognize the essential elements of what later Arab chemists called an alembic still.

Stills were a symbol of alchemy – one is prominent in the right foreground of this 1728 print by Hinrich von Bauditz.

That ancient forerunner may have been used for extracting plant oils for perfume or for alcohol, but as of this writing no tests have been run on the inside of the pot to figure out what was used as a raw material.

Whether the knowledge of the distilling process travelled from India, possibly when Alexander's troops went there, or Greek scientists figured it out themselves, scientists in classical Athens knew about it. Aristotle mentioned it briefly, but there is no evidence that it was used commercially. The Romans did nothing to advance the technology, though many assume they did because of a widely quoted aphorism attributed to the poet Ovid, 'There is more refreshment and stimulation in a nap, even the briefest, than in all the alcohol ever distilled.' Ovid had much to say about the benefits of napping, but this particular statement probably originated with nineteenth-century wit Edward Lucas.

Shortly after the year AD 1000, Avicenna and other alchemists improved the still, using the results as a base for medicines and perfumes. Around 1150 some unknown genius in Europe hit on the idea of lengthening the tube between the boiler and collector in order to cool the vapours. This coil of tubing, called the condenser, vastly improved the efficiency of the alembic still, and created the silhouette of the equipment we know today. The first distilled alcoholic beverages on record were referred as *aqua ardens*, literally 'burning water'. It's a reasonable name for raw alcohol, one that would be repeated in many languages over the centuries.

Brandy was recorded in the early 1300s, whisky and vodka by 1405, and the process of distilling was so common by the Elizabethan era that every manor house had its 'still room' where the women of the house made a beverage they called *aqua vitae*: water of life. While alchemists still strove to use their primitive stills to create a literal elixir of immortality, common people used the same equipment to make medicines and recreational beverages. These were still raw spirits, since the techniques of ageing and mellowing were in their infancy, but they were an exciting development and technicians across the continent worked to refine the craft.

Even Fewer Words about the History of Sugar

People have known for at least 3,000 years that sugar cane, a perennial grass of the genus *Saccharum*, yielded a juice that could be fermented. There is a common misconception that rum got its name from this botanical classification. This can't be true, because Linnaeus did not assign the genus *Saccharum* to sugar cane until 1753, long after rum was first named.

Various wild species of *Saccharum* flourished throughout Southeast Asia, from the Indo-Burmese border region all the way to central China and far into the Pacific islands. The earliest known cultivation seems to have been in New Guinea 6,000 years ago, but it was in India that we have the first written record of the plant's cultivation and fermentation.

A manuscript called the *Manasollana*, or 'Book of the Happy State of Mind', dates from the Vedic period in India around 1800 BC and includes a recipe for sugar-cane beer. More tantalizingly, another manuscript from this period mentions two alcoholic drinks made with sugar, called *soma* and *sura*. *Sura*, made from sugar cane and rice, was given to warriors to enhance their courage. *Soma* was reserved for the aristocracy and credited with promoting positive qualities, but unfortunately we don't know what was in it. (Manuscripts from this period frequently contain words whose exact meaning is unknown, so recreating any recipe from this period is problematic.) Whatever was in *soma*, it was one

This picture shows an acolyte of Krishna drinking alcohol, which the ancient Hindus used as a medicine and sacrament.

of several alcohol-based elixirs that could be found in the medical cabinet of ancient India.

Alexander the Great's troops marvelled at 'honey made without bees', the first description of sugar-cane syrup by an outsider, when they came through the neighbourhood in 326 BC. If any of them took cuttings back to Greece to plant there, they were disappointed; the cane grows poorly in a Mediterranean climate, so sugar was destined to be an exotic and expensive imported item. As early as AD 95, a book on trade through the Red Sea mentioned 'honey from reeds

which is called *sakchar*', the first documented trade in sugar
to Europe.

Muslim traders in the Middle Ages made huge profits in
the sugar trade and introduced the plant to Egypt and Sicily,
which were close to the huge European market. The price
dropped, but profits didn't, since the volume of trade increased

'*Saccharum officindiarum*', etching, from *Hooker's Botanical Miscellany*
(1830–33).

dramatically. Eventually Europeans considered the vast amount of money they were paying to Muslim traders with whom they were at least nominally at war and looked for a place where they could grow sugar cane themselves.

The Portuguese were first with sugar plantations in their African colonies and the Azores, which at first were worked by petty criminals and Jews in a penal environment. That labour force was insufficient and difficult to control, so black Africans were bought from Arab traders and the link between sugar and slavery was born.

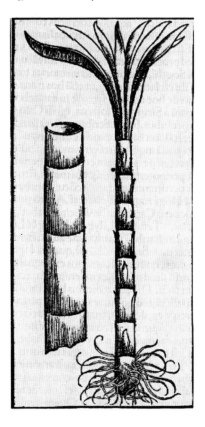

Sugar cane illustration in a Latin edition of Sebastian Münster's *Cosmographia* (Basel, c. 1544).

This Dutch engraving of the slave trade to Brazil by Johannes de Ram of *c.* 1680 shows a white trader who has just paid his native assistant. Note the chains attached to the stone and the African captives behind them.

Though the profits from these ventures were huge, treacherous currents and unpredictable Sahara winds off the African coast made the journey extremely dangerous. The potential for gain having been well established, the powers of Europe looked to the New World to produce this very old crop.

2

The Elusive Origins of Rum:
From the Caribbean to the USA

Just when and where sugar cane first flourished in the Americas is a matter of debate, but there were certainly canefields and sugar mills on the island of Hispaniola by 1516, at Porto Seguro in Brazil by 1520, and in Jamaica, Cuba and Puerto Rico by 1595.

The Portuguese had a technological edge thanks to their experiences in Africa, and applied that knowledge in their vast Brazilian dominion. Portuguese planters in the Brazilian area of São Vicente were reporting huge returns on investment on their plantations by the 1530s, and could have done even better but for chronic labour shortages; the natives would not willingly work the fields and disappeared into the hinterlands, where they easily eluded pursuers. The Portuguese started importing slaves from their colonies in Africa, people who had no hope of blending in with the locals if they escaped, and thus African slavery came to the New World.

The rival empires of Spain, Britain and France all turned to the same source for labour, buying slaves from Arab traders. Sugar plantations took on the look of opulent prisons, with a *casa grande* or manor house where the masters enjoyed whatever imported luxuries were available, and the *senzalas* or slave quarters where their workers lived in squalor. Somewhere in one of these remote outposts, someone who knew the everyday household technique of distilling applied it to either the sugar-cane juice or the sludge left over from sugar processing, and a crude version of the drink we now call rum was born.

Exactly where and when this first happened has been a subject of much debate, and the answer will never be known for sure. Record-keeping on the wild fringes of great empires is often haphazard and confined to essentials, and local administrators were unlikely to regard the fact that someone had brewed a new form of popskull liquor as hot news. Indeed, mentioning to your superiors that people under your command had developed a brand new form of vice could be a career-shortening event. It has been claimed that Dutch Jews in Martinique distilled some sort of liquor from sugar as early as 1550, but the records are too scanty to allow us to draw any conclusions. The first firm documentation is a 1552 report from Governor Tomé de Souza of Bahia in the Portuguese

Cutting sugar cane was excruciating and dangerous in tropical heat. William Clark, 'Slaves cutting the Sugar Cane, 1786', *from Ten Views in the Island of Antigua*, 1786.

The first unequivocal mention of alcohol distilled from sugar in the New World was in this book, published in 1648 by German naturalist George Marcgrave.

colony of Brazil, which mentions that the slaves on sugar plantations were more passive and willing to work if allowed to drink '*cachaco*'. That term is similar to one for alcohol used for pickling rather than drinking, indicating a primitive and rough spirit. The masters in the *casa grande* would certainly have scorned it, preferring wine and brandy imported from Europe. It would also have been their only legal choice, since while the governors of the colony might have ignored the local use of a product made from waste materials if it kept the slaves tractable, the Caribbean and South American colonies were supposed to provide raw materials to the mother country and import all finished products and luxuries. Trade between colonies – or, even worse, between colonies and foreigners – was strictly prohibited. The fortunes of many among the Spanish and Portuguese aristocracy were based on commerce in brandy and wines, and they wanted no competition from other sources, even from within their own colonies. If alcohol made from sugar had been seen as any threat to those very profitable monopolies, its manufacture would have been suppressed – as the Portuguese government tried to do as early as 1639. In 1647 – before the first mention of any beverage distilled from sugar anywhere else – the Portuguese government ordered that only slaves were allowed to drink cachaça, though it was permitted to sell it to residents of Pernambuco, which was then under Dutch rule. The Portuguese government regarded rum as a health hazard and a nuisance, but evidently didn't mind exporting a social problem to their commercial rivals.

There are no conclusive records of rum distilling in the Spanish or French Caribbean in this era, but it is hard to believe that it didn't happen. Distillation was an everyday skill in both cultures and there were hundreds of sugar plantations around the islands and South American mainland; it strains credibility that nobody but the Portuguese ever thought to try running some molasses or cane juice through a still to see what happened. The French cleric Jean-Baptiste Du Tertre brought a still to Martinique in 1650 and experimented with it during his eight-year stay on the island, but rum was apparently not a common beverage there for some years afterward. The Dutch were experienced distillers and produced sugar on the Caribbean islands they owned, which makes it even more surprising that they never developed much of a rum trade.

The first mention of rum from the Caribbean is both famous and derogatory: the report from a visitor to the British colony of Barbados in 1651 that mentioned that 'The chief fuddling they make in the island is *Rumbullion*, alias *Kill-Divil*, and this is made of sugar canes distilled, a hot, hellish, and terrible liquor.' This is the first recorded use of any variant of the term 'rum', and is cited by many historians as the

This map of Barbados from 1657 shows the principal sugar plantations and also (at the top) a mounted man shooting at runaway slaves.

date of the invention of liquor distilled from sugar. The misconception lives on, and the connection with Barbados was sufficiently strong in English-speaking regions that rum was called Barbadoes-Liquor throughout the eighteenth century.

The origin of the name 'rumbullion' is hotly disputed, with some partisans alleging that the word 'rum' was rustic British slang for 'excellent'. Others point to an alleged link between the words 'rum' and 'scrum', meaning fight, or 'rumbustious', meaning exuberant, noisy and undisciplined. Given that every first-hand report of rum from this era emphasizes how raw and awful it was, the 'excellent' explanation seems far fetched. There is a well-documented propensity for rum drinkers of the period to fight, and this etymology seems more likely.

(Many early references to rum in free populations remark how people who drink it are inclined to violence, while slaves were more tractable when they drank it. Surely there is no inherent quality in rum that makes it have these diametrically opposed effects in different populations. It seems more likely that those who have no hope of freedom drink themselves into an apathetic stupor and are less likely to run riot than free people in newly settled communities with little supervision.)

The adjective 'kill-devil' was at least as popular a name as rum for many years, and in fact became the vernacular term for it in Dutch (*keelduivel*) and French (*gueldive*). No report or description of rum would refer to it as a beverage fit for gentlemen for almost a hundred years.

The British Commercialize Rum

Unlike the French, Portuguese and Spanish, the British had no indigenous wine and brandy trade to protect, and the colonial administration allowed the making of rum and its export to other British colonies. Entrepreneurs started trading in rum as soon as they figured out how to make it, though it seems that smuggling became a problem almost immediately. An order from the Governor and Council of Jamaica from the Calendar of State Papers Colonial in 1661 ordained 'that the former orders concerning rum, sugar, and hammocks be still in force, viz., one half to be forfeited to the King, and one half to the informer.' What any informer would do with half a hammock is a question that is left unanswered. It is unfortunate that the date and text of that previous order is unknown, since it was the first attempt by the British to regulate a smuggling trade that quickly became notorious.

All early references to rum describe it as a public nuisance and social evil. In 1661 Governor Robert Hooper of Barbados ordered soldiers to close 'sundry small houses for selling rum', one of a long list of actions designed to increase order in the community. In 1670 a Barbados merchant named John Style sent an extended rant to the colonial overlords in Whitehall, alleging that

> The number of tippling houses is now doubly increased, so that there is not now resident upon this place ten men to every house that selleth strong liquors. There are more than 100 licensed houses, besides sugar and rum works that sell without license; and what can that bring but ruin, for many sell their plantations, and either go out for privateers, or drinking themselves into debt, sell their bodies or are sold for prison fees.

There is no evidence that any action was taken, or that Styles even received a reply. He was not alone in his complaints of rampant alcoholism, and the next year Governor West of Barbados, in a requisition for supplies, said he hoped that

> their Honours are thinking of sending a supply [of servants] from England, for some will be out of their time next year, and one English servant is worth two Barbadians, for they are so much addicted to rum that they will do little but while the bottle is at their nose.

The fortune of Governor West's colony was based on molasses and the rum trade, but there was a price to be paid in efficiency.

Though it is doubtful that Barbados deserves the often-claimed title of 'birthplace of rum', it was certainly the first place that rum was commercialized and turned to a more refined drink. As in many other trading ventures, the entrepreneurial British took inefficient and languishing markets and turned them into profitable concerns. The planters of Brazil made a primitive and foul version of rum for 70 years without improving it or merchandizing it; the same class of people in Barbados refined the spirit and turned it into a money machine within a decade of its first appearance on their shores.

Rum in New England

British rum was not widely traded outside the Caribbean at this time, but molasses, the raw material, soon found a ready market in New England. The earliest mention of rum in New England is from 1657, when the General Court of Massachusetts declared the overproduction of alcohol, 'whether knowne by the name of rumme, strong water, wine, brandy, etc., etc.', a menace to society. Since this law addresses an existing trade and the process of legislation was slow, rum must have been sold there for some time. By 1667 that same body took action against innkeepers who sold weak beer fortified with rum.

Rum was certainly made in Staten Island, New York, by 1664, in Boston by 1667 and in Philadelphia by 1671. Doctors of the period considered the liquor to be medicinal, believing that the air and water of America's 'hot climate' were unwholesome. Rum had its medicinal purpose on cold, damp days too – it was drunk just before leaving the house as an 'antifogmatick' to ward off the chill. Rum was drunk to prevent the evil effects of this environment, and while it may have done little to alleviate other malaises, it certainly did much to stimulate the economy. Unlike the sparsely forested Caribbean islands, where fuel was expensive, New England had vast forests to supply the fires of the distilleries. Its workforce also included many Scots and Irish, who had learned the trade in their mother countries. The cool northern climate made spending days among the fires of a distillery more tolerable than the hellish occupation it was in the Caribbean, and well-charted currents made transportation routine and inexpensive.

Molasses quickly became part of colonial culture. It had many uses in cooking and baking by honest housewives, including 'Indian Pudding', made from corn, molasses and butter. In 1671 the pioneer doctor and botanist John Josselyn remarked that he was served molasses-beer made with sassafras root, water and bran in Maine; this is one of the first references to a fermented but undistilled sugar-cane product in North America. Josselyn made a distinction between this sugar beer and rum, and recommended the latter boiled together with onions as a treatment for gout and kidney stones. Those who tried this remedy would be denied the anaesthetic qualities of the rum, since Josselyn prescribed boiling the rum and onions into a plaster and applying it to the patient's hip.

As the production of rum took hold, it became a central ingredient of the hot toddies that warmed and comforted people through freezing winters. Some of these were elaborate in preparation; a man known as Landlord May of Canton, Massachusetts, became famous for a concoction that began with sugar, eggs and cream left to stand for two days. This was added to a mug of beer that was heated with a hot poker, with a gill of rum tossed into the creamy mixture just before serving to finish it off. (This may sound odd but it is actually delicious, like an alcoholic marshmallow. You can find the recipe for this and other rum drinks at the back of this book.) The same drink with an egg beaten into it just before serving was called 'bellows-top', and had a consistency almost like custard.

There were other combinations of rum with 'hard' (or alcoholic) cider, the most popular beverage of New England, and with molasses and spruce beer to create a beverage with the delightful named *callibogus*. Another popular drink of the period was rum shrub, a cordial made with sugar, vinegar and orange or lime juice. (This usage of the word 'shrub' probably comes from the Arabic *sharab*, to drink, not from the word for a small bush.) The vinegar gives shrubs a tart flavour and makes them exceptionally refreshing, a sophisticated cocktail from colonial days.

Those who cared more about effect than aesthetics drank rum straight, which was usually regarded as a sign of desperation or depravity. Puritans naturally disliked this recreational beverage, and in 1686 Increase Mather preached one of his typically aggrieved sermons against it. 'It is an unhappy thing that in later years a kind of drink called Rum has been common

The author stirs a jug of Landlord May's Flip with a hot poker to caramelize the sugars and boil the mixture of beer, rum, egg, cream and sugar.

among us. They that are poor, and wicked too, can for a penny or two-pence make themselves drunk.'

Rum was cheap because the raw materials were inexpensive and highly productive; a gallon of imported molasses and some water would make a gallon of rum. In 1673 molasses could be bought for one shilling a gallon, and the rum made from it sold for six shillings per gallon – an enviable profit for very little work. As the trade grew in volume the price fell, and rum was made on an industrial scale and exported widely.

New England seamen and merchants conducted this trade while living under laws that restricted the drinking of alcoholic beverages in highly intrusive ways. As Josselyn complained,

> at the houses of entertainment called ordinaries into which a stranger went, he was presently followed by one appointed to that office who would thrust himself into his company uninvited, and if he called for more drink than the officer thought, in his judgment, he could soberly bear away, he would presently countermand it, and appoint the proportion beyond which he could not get one drop.

Anyone who managed to get enough alcohol to get drunk faced fines and humiliation, including a day in the stocks and having to wear a red D around his neck for a month afterward. These restrictions were even greater for Native Americans, and beginning in 1633 anyone selling rum to them could be fined. These restrictions seemed harsh to the easygoing New Yorkers, who opined that 'to prohibit all strong liquor to them seems very hard and very turkish, rumm doth as little hurt as the ffrenchmans Brandie, and in the whole is much more wholesome.' They were alone in their charitable concern for the Native Americans' right to drink; most others of the period expressed fear of a rebellion of 'inflamed devilish bloody savages'. The tribes themselves were divided on the issue, some chiefs recognizing the social problems of drunkenness among their people. In 1695, when an invasion by the French was expected, the chief of the Onondaga tribe asked Governor Fletcher to 'discharge the selling of rum to any of our nations. Let them have powder and lead instead of rum.' Other chiefs took a different view; in 1763, Seneca chief Wabbicomicot demanded rum from the soldiers at Fort Niagara, warning that he could not guarantee peace with his people if they remained sober. Benjamin Franklin recorded a native orator who proclaimed:

> The Great Spirit, who made all things, made every thing for some use, and whatever use he design'd any thing for, that use it should always be put to. Now, when he made rum, he said 'Let this be for the Indians to get drunk with,' and it must be so.

Franklin added his own gloomy note afterwards:

> And, indeed, if it be the design of Providence to extirpate these savages in order to make room for cultivators of the earth, it seems not improbable that rum may be the appointed means. It has already annihilated all the tribes who formerly inhabited the sea-coast.

The rum that so destroyed the culture of the Native Americans was made locally in New England, where new technologies for industrial distilling made high volumes possible. As usually happens, high volume led to low prices; as Burke put it later,

> The quantity of spirits which they distill in Boston from the molasses they import is as surprising as the cheapness at which they sell it, which is under two shillings a gallon; but they are more famous for the quantity and cheapness than for the excellency of their rum.

This picture of 1823 shows the idealized British industry – impeccably dressed overseers supervising hard-working slaves. On the left are the stills; on the right are windmills for grinding cane.

Superior rums came from the Caribbean, particularly Barbados, where improved distilling technology was aided by the tropical heat. Spirits mellow much more quickly in warm weather, so even if New Englanders had followed the same procedures, their rum would not have matched those imported from the West Indies. A tiered pricing system quickly developed, with West Indian rum priced at twice the cost of New England rum. Inferior products still sold in vast quantities for mixing into compound beverages, consumption by the lower classes, and for trading for slaves.

By 1686 the Southern colonies were buying New England rum in quantity, and it quickly became a form of currency. All colonies were chronically short of money and often had to resort to barter, since Britain had prohibited the export of silver coins. This led to the widespread use of Spanish, French and Dutch coins, as well as the Austrian

Thaler from which American currency gets its name, but there were still not enough in circulation.

Rum filled the vacuum: it could easily be measured and divided, and then either drunk by the recipient or traded again for something else. Wages were paid in rum as early as October 1700, when the New York council specified that the carpenters building a pinnace for the customs service were to be given rum as part of their wages. (That small, fast vessel would be used to chase rum-smugglers, so one hopes that the liquor the carpenters were paid with was obtained legally.) This practice became so commonplace that the great economist Adam Smith later mentioned it in *The Wealth of Nations*:

> In the province of New York, common labourers earn three shillings and sixpence currency, equal to two shillings sterling, a day; ship carpenters, ten shillings and sixpence currency, with a pint of rum worth sixpence sterling, equal in all to six shillings and sixpence sterling.

In time larger transactions and contracts specified rum for payment, a practice that quickly spread beyond New England. The first piece of land to change hands in Kernersville, North Carolina, which is over 200 miles inland, was priced at four gallons of rum.

Rum Smuggling and the Triangle Trade

The habit of paying in rum was a headache for administrators and tax collectors. In November 1690 Collector of Customs Edward Randolph reported that residents of Virginia and North Carolina were smuggling the majority of the tobacco they produced, and on the rare occasions when they were caught, they paid the duty in rum. Randolph's reports were notoriously biased against the colonists, and his opinion of their beverages may be discerned from the final paragraph of a letter he wrote home:

> I am indisposed, not finding agreeable diet or drink. I have not been accustomed to rum. *Signed*, Ed. Randolph. Please to excuse the writing, the matter is too true.

Whatever his opinion of the colonists and their beverages, there's no denying that rum-smuggling had become a global business by the end of the seventeenth century. In July 1699 Governor Coote of New York wrote:

> 'Tis the most beneficial trade, that to Madagascar with the pirates, that ever was heard of, and I believe there's more got that way than by turning pirates and robbing. I am told this Shelley sold rum, which cost but 2*s.* per gallon at N. York, for 50*s.* and £3 per gallon at Madagascar.

To the consternation of the upright locals, respectable citizens were sometimes caught engaged in this illicit trade, which was lubricated by gifts of rum to customs inspectors who were less than diligent about their work after sampling it. Even prominent citizens were caught smuggling: Peter Faneuil of Boston (after whom Faneuil Hall is named) had one of his ships seized in 1736 for illegally trading with the French. He was practising other ruses in the liquor trade too: a letter to his French agent surfaced, advising him to 'See what good French brandy is worth, and if it be possible to cloak it and ship it for rum.'

Just what percentage of rum was smuggled can never be known, but there were many entrepreneurs operating along a vast and lightly patrolled coast, and the officials in charge of suppressing the trade were notoriously bribable. All the official statistics of the economic effect of the rum trade are undoubtedly underestimations. Rum and the molasses used to make it were the most heavily traded commodities in the Caribbean by 1700, and the main source of profit for Britain's colonial enterprise in the Americas.

Rum also fuelled what came to be known as the Triangle Trade, in which molasses was exported to New England to be made into rum; rum to Africa to trade for slaves; and slaves to the Caribbean and South America to produce sugar for molasses. (The same ships did not travel to all three points of the triangle, since slave ships were not ideal for other cargo, but that is the way the money flowed.)

Rum was not responsible for the African slave trade, which the Arabs had conducted since at least the thirteenth century, but that trade expanded exponentially when it was discovered that sugar cane was a crop that could be easily harvested from huge plantations by forced labour. As the voyages became routine, the volume of trade increased and became more specialized. The islands of the British Caribbean exported sugar and molasses and imported everything else, becoming dependent on faraway places for staple foods. Grain, cattle and vegetable cultivation withered in the Caribbean, because sugar cane cultivation brought in more money.

Even such occupations as fishing in the rich Caribbean waters were forsaken in pursuit of increased rum production. A brief entry from the journal of Emmanuel Downing reads, 'Leader has cast the iron pans to be used in the process. Frequent commerce with the West Indies carried out, unmerchantable fish to be exchanged for molasses.' Since molasses was a waste product of sugar refining, what we see documented here is the dregs of the fishing trade being

exchanged for the dregs of the sugar trade, to the benefit of both parties. The results of this trade route are still plain in cuisines all over the Caribbean, where cod is popular even though that coldwater fish would die in the warm ocean. Caribbean islanders who are the descendants of slaves still celebrate with codfish fritters; and though the raw material for these is no longer traded for human beings, it is still paid for with profits from rum.

That enterprise received a huge boost in 1655 when the British captured Jamaica from the Spanish. The soil and climate of that island were excellent for growing sugar cane, it was over twenty times larger than Barbados, and unlike Barbados it had both fuel and water in abundance. Planters and slaves poured in, distilleries were established and Jamaican rum quickly became esteemed as the standard of quality. The

This Jamaican stamp from 1956 reveals the reason the British considered Jamaica such a prize – it shows Queen Elizabeth framed by sugar cane stalks.

population of Jamaica quadrupled within two decades as new plantations were founded, and eventually slaves out-numbered free people by twenty to one. The city of Port Royal became famously wicked and wealthy, and until an earthquake destroyed it in 1692 it was a crossroads for the whole Caribbean.

Slavery also flourished in the islands of the French Caribbean, where some attempts were made to establish humane standards of treatment. The Code Noir of 1717 prohibited planters giving their slaves tafia (French slang for low-quality rum) instead of food. This law was regularly violated, and there are many reports of slaves who had Sundays off, but spent the Lord's day bartering rum in order to support their families.

Until Great Britain outlawed the slave trade in 1807, it was a multinational affair, though in theory the planters were supposed to buy slaves transported by their own country-men. Though the slave trade was dominated by British ships even after slavery became illegal, American, Dutch and French ships also engaged in it. An accurate assessment of the trade is impossible because so much of it was illicit; after a certain point we can only make guesses and extrapolations based on the records of prosecution of those who were caught.

There were profits from the Triangle Trade for everyone but the slaves who were bought and sold. The fortunes to be made from the sale of rum became proverbial. Richard Cumberland's play *The West-Indian* of 1770 featured a title character who was said to control 'enough sugar and rum to turn the Thames into a rum-punch'. Samuel Morewood, writing in 1838, estimated that the rum made from a Jamaican plantation in this era covered all of the expenses of the operation, so that all the sugar produced was pure profit. Genteel families of the era preferred to ignore the slavery at the root of their wealth; in Jane Austen's *Mansfield Park* (1814), the wealthy Sir Thomas Bertram departs for a year to deal with problems on his plantation in Antigua. While he is absent, Austen's heroine Fanny Price asks one of the family about the conditions of slaves on his plantations. The response is a

Though this engraving of a distillery dates from 1823, the techniques were the same as an earlier era. Here slaves fill hogsheads with rum while a cooper makes barrels and a white manager looks on.

Wilberforce's movement called attention to slavery using sugar bowls like this one, which bears the inscription 'East India Sugar not made by Slaves'.

dead silence; such topics were obviously not appropriate to polite society. Fanny and the rest of the company quickly return to more important topics, such as the arrangements for their next party.

Mansfield Park was popular at the very time that the British public began to regard the slave trade as both a corrupting influence and immoral by nature. The charismatic politician William Wilberforce expounded eloquently on the evils of slavery; on the lighter side, satiric poet William Cowper penned a famous verse in 1788 called 'Pity for Poor Africans':

> I own I am shock'd at the purchase of slaves,
> And fear those who buy them and sell them are knaves;
> What I hear of their hardships, their tortures, and groans,
> Is almost enough to draw pity from stones.

I pity them greatly, but I must be mum,
For how could we do without sugar and rum?

Whether converted by Wilberforce's eloquence, Cowper's satire or the gentle persuasion of prominent Quakers, many Englishmen took to ostentatiously refusing to use Caribbean sugar, preferring sugar from India made by free people. Trafficking in slaves from Africa was abolished in 1806, and slavery was abolished throughout the British Empire in 1833. The social upheaval in the Caribbean was considerable, with African former slaves disinclined to work on the plantations, or in some places actually barred from working there as free men, and plantation owners turned to importing labourers from India. Though these workers toiled in conditions that a modern worker would find intolerable, they were much better than those experienced by slaves, and the free labour force turned out to be more productive. The eventual result was that despite worldwide competition, the British Caribbean continued to produce both the highest volume of rum and the best-quality rum. They could not have foreseen it, but they were increasing their output just as changes in taste, civil war in America and other factors were about to lead to a reduction in demand.

3
Rum Manufacture by Other European Powers

Though Jane Austen's characters and thousands of enterprising Britons made vast fortunes from rum, entrepreneurs from other countries were forbidden to follow their example. The Spanish prohibited the manufacture of rum in their vast holdings, citing the protection of public health and morals, and the ban was only lifted in 1796. The administrators of their colonial enterprise were obsessed with the gold and silver of Mexico and Peru, so little attention was given to the sugar trade and none to rum.

The Portuguese oscillated between grudging toleration and suppression. Illicit trade was apparently widespread between Brazil and the Portuguese colony of Angola, and in the year 1659 the authorities in Lisbon ordered the destruction of all stills in Brazil together with all ships caught trafficking in illegal alcohol. The official reason given was that productivity of the gold mines in the colony was unacceptably low because the workers were drunk on cachaça. The prohibition sparked what came to be known as the Cachaça Rebellion of 1660, a revolt that resulted in the city of Rio de Janeiro being governed by rebels for five months. This was the first rebellion against a colonial power in South American history, and the Portuguese government eventually relented and allowed rum to be produced, though it was not permitted to export it.

After the Cachaça Rebellion rum was legalized for a while, but almost all trade was to Africa in exchange for slaves. Since Brazil produced huge quantities of gold and diamonds and the sugar trade there was profitable by itself, the commercial potential of rum was ignored. In 1744 the government of John II outlawed the making of cachaça again, and though small-scale manufacture continued, export ceased for almost 60 years. Cachaça was legalized and taxed heavily after the Lisbon Earthquake of 1755, when the government in Portugal was in desperate need of funds to rebuild.

The people who actually harvested sugar cane probably did not look as glamorous as the person depicted on this bottle of Negro Old Rum from Martinique.

The French occupied some of the best islands in the Caribbean for growing cane, and at first they had better distilling technology and more mastery of the technique. However, a combination of prejudice and government restriction assured that export was limited and the products inferior. Rum was recorded in Martinique as early as 1667, called *eau-de-vie, gueldive* or tafia. It was made by and for slaves. Distiller and cleric Jean Labat employed only women at the distillery he called the *vinegarie*, believing that, unlike men, they could be trusted not to get drunk. Local merchants and administrators saw the vast potential for profit from the rum trade, and Dutch and Jewish artisans made some quality rum, but the government in Paris was unmoved and outlawed its manufacture in 1713. Labat pointed out in detail just how much potential profit was being forfeited, but in vain.

There were substantial smuggling operations in the French Caribbean colonies, but the export industry did not mature until rum was fully legalized in the 1770s. By then other changes were taking place that ensured that the French never caught up with their British rivals.

There was one place where the French laws against the rum trade were ignored from the beginning, though it was not the best place for growing the raw materials. Sugar cane flourishes in the islands of the Caribbean, but was a marginal crop on the North American mainland; the sudden freezes that can hit even Florida and Texas devastated the strains that were then cultivated. The Company of the Indies, the French colonial administrators of the colony, planted cane in Louisiana as early as 1720 but suffered crop failures as often as one year in three. What sugar they made was shipped back to France, but as time went by an increasing amount of the cane juice was made into tafia. The first history of Louisiana, written by Governor Du Pratt, makes several references to tafia, usually as a beverage for slaves. There were intermittent attempts to regulate the trade, such as the 1757 law prohibiting the sale of tafia to slaves and soldiers, the two groups with whom it was most popular. Tafia eventually caught on among all classes in New Orleans, and in 1764 Governor Jean Jacques d'Abadie noted sadly that 'The immoderate use of tafia has stupefied the whole population.'

Only a year later, France ceded Louisiana to Spain, but the Spanish governors had only a tenuous hold on the colony and made no serious attempt to suppress the rum business. The trade received a boost in about 1781 when Joseph Solis arrived from Cuba with cane cuttings that turned out to be both cold-tolerant and highly productive. Solis was also a talented horticulturist, and figured out ways to improve previously marginal operations. Around 1784 Solis did something highly unusual: he opened a crushing mill that, according to historian Charles Gayarre, 'made molasses and tafia (a distilled drink) from the cane juice, but no sugar'. This

John Hinton's 1749 print of sugar-making in the West Indies shows all the stages of production.

is the first instance I have been able to find of any operation that focused on making rum and regarded crystalline sugar as a by-product.

Joseph Solis made plenty of money from his distillery, selling most of his output at the tavern his father Manuel ran in New Orleans. The Spanish rulers of a mostly French population ignored his establishment and others like them, except in 1785, when Governor Esteban Rodríguez Miró demanded that taverns be closed during divine services on Sunday. Even this modest restriction was ignored, and rum-drinking continued to flourish in New Orleans. We have few independent reports of the quality of this rum, but it was good enough that in 1798 4,000 casks of 50 gallons each were shipped up the Mississippi to the Ohio river valley. The market for Spanish and French rum was there, but the will and skill to commercialize the trade was not.

This failure to legalize and encourage trade had long-lasting effects. The technology of rum manufacturing improved by leaps and bounds in places ruled by the British, thanks to improved stills and experience of ageing techniques, but other colonies turned out the same liquor that was so vilified when it was first invented. It sold cheaply and illegally, when it sold at all, and taxes were not collected by colonial administrations. They were consequently poorer then their British competitors, and destined to fall even further behind as the rum trade increased. It was a deliberate abandonment of an obviously lucrative business, and a blunder of vast proportions.

Rum and the American Revolution

French and Spanish plantation owners were eager to cash in on the popularity of rum, and they did so in the only way they

★

PILGRIM RUM

distilled by

FELTON & SON
INCORPORATED
BOSTON · MASS.

Established 1819
Oldest Distillers of Rum in the U.S.

could: by selling the raw material to anyone who would buy it. The French government prohibited the export of rum from their colonies in 1715 in order to protect their market for brandy. This effectively made rum not worth the effort to make and molasses worthless unless someone was interested in buying it on the black market. Many people were, and they were American distillers.

Molasses flowed northward to the New England colonies, frustrating the feeble attempts of tax collectors to police a vast coastline. The British tried to suppress this trade with more vigorous enforcement, but eventually decided that if they couldn't catch the smugglers, they would tax the buyers. The Molasses Act of 1733 put a tax of sixpence per gallon on molasses imported from non-British colonies, which if collected would have more than doubled the price of French Caribbean molasses. This tax was explicitly designed to enrich the British Caribbean planters at the expense of the New Englanders, whose prosperity was seen as provoking a movement for separation from the Empire. When Martin Bladen, a member of the British Board of Trade, was asked about the likely economic effects on the New Englanders, he replied that

> The duties proposed would not prove an absolute prohibition, but [Bladen] meant them as something that should come very near it, for in the way the northern colonies are, they raise the French Islands at the expense of ours, and raise themselves also too high, even to an independency.

Predictably, the New Englanders continued smuggling, bribing inspectors and intimidating tax collectors, and the tax raised little revenue and much ill will. It eventually created exactly the circumstances it sought to avoid: the obvious corruption of colonial officials and widespread avoidance of the tax encouraged colonial thoughts of independence. In 1754 one of the architects of the revolution ran for election in the Virginia House of Burgesses. At one event his campaign manager served up 28 gallons of rum, 50 gallons of rum punch, 34 gallons of wine, 46 gallons of beer and two gallons of cider. (Note that gallon measures in this era are approximate as standards varied depending on regions; measures were only standardized in 1824 in the British Empire, 1899 in the USA.) It may be suspected that not all of the rum at this event was made from legal products. The politician in question, one George Washington by name, won handily and went on to even greater things.

A prohibitively high tax having proved unsuccessful at suppressing illegal molasses, the Board of Trade decided to withdraw it and levy a tax that would allow some profit to the Americans. The Sugar Act of 1764 reduced the tax to three pence per gallon of molasses, but required that most processed items could only be exported to Britain, where they fetched much lower prices. The effect was to make the inferior New England rum even less competitive with that of the Caribbean, where Britain's colonies were more dependent and tractable. The rampant discontent caused by the Sugar Act led to sporadic violence and the first organized boycotts of British luxury goods. The revolutionary movement did not ignite until the Stamp Act was passed the following year, but the fuse had been lit by the tax on rum.

Once the revolution actually began, the Americans were cut off from their usual suppliers in Jamaica and Barbados and dependent on French and Spanish molasses. One estimate states that the average adult male in the colonies drank between four and five gallons of rum per year, so local distillers were in a panic to produce enough to fill demand. The quality of New England rum, always low, became even worse, and whiskey became cheaper and more popular. In time whiskey-drinking came to be seen as patriotic, since it was made from local materials and hence all profit stayed in America. Rum was not a part of the military rations approved by Congress in 1775, but many officers paid for rum for their men as a way of slowing the rate of desertions. The availability of so much alcohol among poorly trained and undisciplined troops caused problems with fighting. Lieutenant James McMichael wryly recorded instances of a disease he called barrel fever, 'which differs in its effects from any other fever – its concomitants are black eyes and bloody noses'.

Rum was directly involved with one of the most famous incidents of the war: Washington's crossing of the Delaware to surprise and capture Hessian troops at Christmas of 1776. The return crossing was considerably delayed because despite Washington's orders to destroy the Hessians' rum, his men drank it and got so inebriated that many fell out of their boats. The Father of his Country had read Paine's lines 'These are the times that try men's souls' to his soldiers in camp a few days earlier; this must have been a time that tried the general's own patience. Washington certainly understood the morale-building effect of rum – he supplied a ration to all his troops in March 1777 to reward them for surviving the dreadful winter in Valley Forge. The British made fun of the American troops' alleged fondness for alcohol, as in this lyric from 'Yankee Doodle's Expedition to Rhode Island':

> So Yankee Doodle did forget, the sound of British
>   drum, sir.
> How oft it made him quake and sweat, in spite of
>   Yankee rum, sir.

The soldiers on both sides of the conflict expected rations of alcohol, and morale suffered when they didn't get it, so running low on liquor was a matter of anxiety among quartermasters. When the British general William Tryon raided the Continental Army storehouse at Danbury, Connecticut, in April 1777, he ordered his soldiers to burn 120 barrels of rum. Tryon's soldiers were every bit as undisciplined as Washington's. They drank as much as they could before setting the rest afire, and burned the entire town afterwards.

Following the end of the revolutionary war in 1781, trade between the new country and the British Caribbean was cut off for more than a decade, and distillers relied on molasses from Spanish and French islands. Americans continued distilling, their domestic market strengthened because no legal rum came in from British colonies, and the rum available from French and Spanish colonies was often inferior to their own. As President, George Washington served Madeira wine, whiskey and rum at official functions, and his wife Martha's rum punch recipe can be found later in this book. When the Washingtons retired to Mount Vernon he operated a distillery, and though he made whiskey, he kept up a lively correspondence about techniques with another gentleman farmer who made rum. The period from 1781 until 1790, when slave revolts in Haiti disrupted commerce with the French Caribbean, represented the peak of legal commerce between America and the French Caribbean. After that successful revolt other islands competed to fill the void; the Spanish legalized slavery in Cuba only one year after Haiti

This scene of dancing in an American tavern shows a peaceful, jolly side of a maligned institution. Note the kegs marked 'Rum' behind the bar and the picture of George Washington on the wall.

declared independence in order to provide a steady source of labour for their own sugar plantations.

The French molasses trade was further disrupted when the Napoleonic Wars caused chaos throughout the Caribbean, and British expeditions captured many French islands. The entry of the USA into the War of 1812 caused prices to rise so that New England rum distilleries became even less competitive. The industry began a long decline, hastened by the rising popularity of American whiskey. Though rum distilling was no longer a major occupation in New England, many companies lasted until the Prohibition era. The last rummery in Massachusetts, Felton & Son of Boston, closed its doors in 1983, ending a tradition that had lasted for over 200 years. Craft distillers have opened in Boston in recent years, some with names very similar to bygone brands, but they have no actual connection to the old companies.

One other outpost of rum distilling remained active in North America, in a region utterly unsuited to sugar-cane cultivation. Fishermen in Newfoundland had been trading codfish for molasses since the early 1600s, and the Newfoundlanders made strong, harsh, heavily flavoured rum that has come to be known as Screech. Though made by the same processes that are used to make other rums, it was so awful that rumours spread that it had been adulterated with cleaning products. It got its name during the Second World War, when an unwary American naval officer tossed back a tumbler of it and made a noise that could only be called a screech. Screech is still sold in Newfoundland, but these days most of it is made in Jamaica under contract.

Rum and Piracy

Wherever you find fortunes made honestly, you will find other people attempting to get just as rich without the bother of actually working. Since rum functioned as a de facto currency, traded by ships sailing long distances through poorly charted waters, it was natural that pirates and privateers became interested in hijacking their cargoes. Ships loaded with rum might be less likely to put up a strong resistance, because in a hot Caribbean climate, with many barrels of evaporating alcohol in an enclosed space, any spark in the hold could lead to an explosion.

Rum was the everyday drink of the rough crews of sailing ships, routinely distributed before battles and other tribulations. A page from the pirate Blackbeard's diary from 1718, found aboard his sloop *Adventure*, sums it up better than anything else:

> Such a day; rum all out. Our company somewhat sober; a damned confusion amongst us! Rogues a plotting. Talk of separation. So I looked sharp for a prize [and] took one with a great deal of liquor aboard. So kept the company hot, damned hot, then all things went well again.

Blackbeard was said to drink flaming rum just to intimidate people. If he did, he was probably the most sober man present, since the majority of the alcohol would have burned off. (That a man with a luxuriant moustache and beard would develop the habit of drinking flaming beverages is only one of several reasons to question his sanity.) He also reportedly mixed his rum with gunpowder, a combination that sometimes happened accidentally when the same barrels were used for both commodities.

The few records we have of life among pirate crews often show a similar dependence on rum, as well as a cynical sense of humour. When the pirate captain Thomas Anstis conducted a hasty trial of a captured rival, he appointed an 'Attorney General' from his crew. The prosecutor, having made a poor and rambling speech, concluded with:

> My Lord, I should have spoke much finer than I do now, but as your Lordship knows our rum is all out, and how should a man speak good law that has not drunk a dram? However, I hope your lordship will order the fellow to be hang'd.

Despite the prosecutor's admitted deficiency in oratory, the defendant was found guilty with the anticipated results,

In 1723 pirate Edward Low gave a captured captain a choice: drink punch with him as an equal, or be shot. Woodcut from *The Pirates Own Book* (1837).

and presumably the entire company later found a way to quench their thirst. The story of Anstis and his kangaroo court was printed in sensationalist newspapers and may have been exaggerated for effect, but there are plenty of documents that back up the link between rum and brigandage.

Given the perils that faced even a well-run ship in an era of rudimentary charts and primitive navigation instruments, it seems remarkable that a boatload of belligerent drunks was dangerous to anybody but themselves. There are records of ships being wrecked or run aground by drunken steersmen or crews, such as the incident in 1669 when the buccaneer Sir Henry Morgan lost his flagship because celebrating sailors accidentally lit the powder magazine on fire.

The ancient reputation of rum as a drink for fighting men was burnished by lurid accounts in the popular press, as well as court documents. According to the confessions of the crew of the brig *William*, who in 1829 were hanged for piracy along with their captain, Charles Delano, before every attack the skipper shared out large amounts of rum to put the crew in a fighting mood.

Many other pirates suffered the same fate as the crew of *William*: by 1830 the colonial powers in the Caribbean were cooperating to suppress buccaneers, and the dawn of sophisticated naval gunnery and steam propulsion gave governments an overwhelming advantage over their adversaries.

Jolly Tars and Navy Rum

When it came to imbibing, hard-drinking pirate crews were sometimes evenly matched with their law-abiding counterparts, since sailors on merchant vessels were notorious for tapping any rum in the cargo while officers weren't looking.

Captains ignored small thefts, reasoning that a reputation for harsh discipline raised the likelihood of experienced crew jumping ship in the next port. British and French merchant captains were broadly regarded as tolerant of drinking, Americans more strict. This may have been for business reasons, since by 1850 insurance companies in the US offered cheaper rates to captains who ran a dry ship. Since the insurance adjusters were far away on land while the ships were at sea, some shipowners paid the cheap rates while the crews surreptitiously drank their accustomed tot.

However low the acceptable standards of sobriety, some crewmen couldn't meet them, and were thrown off in strange ports because they were habitual drunks. The vocabulary of sailors reflects this. A 'rum-gagger' was the name for a con man who told stories of his sufferings at sea to obtain money for drinks. Another nautical term related to rum is in more common use: 'rummage' was the name for intrusive searches by customs officials looking for smuggled barrels.

In time the taste for rum spread beyond merchant ships and those who preyed upon them to the British Navy. The Admiralty originally favoured rations of brandy for their crews, but after the capture of Jamaica from the Spanish in 1655, rum was substituted. The logic was obvious: brandy had to be purchased in Europe from the Spanish or French, unreliable allies at the best of times, while rum was produced by British subjects in their own colonies. Buying from those colonists stopped the flow of money to rivals, assured a steady supply regardless of politics, and saved money besides. In 1730 the ration was standardized at half a pint (288 ml) per day of rum exceeding 80 per cent alcohol, and later this was mixed with water or weak beer to create the beverage known as grog. The reason for the name is disputed, but it is usually cited as a reference to Admiral

There's plenty of
Old St. Croix at your
favorite store

A natty and clean-shaven pirate is unusually helpful in this *Fortune* magazine
ad from 1943.

Edward Vernon, whose nickname was Old Grog. Vernon
ordered that rum be diluted to half strength to combat
drunkenness, and later ordered the addition of lemon or
lime juice to mask the foul taste of water that had been
stored in barrels for months. The sailors disliked the new
drink at first, fearing that quartermasters would stint on their
rum rations, but after a short period it became obvious that
Vernon's sailors were far healthier than those who continued

drinking straight rum. This was actually because the vitamin c in the juice reduced the risk of scurvy, but at the time this wasn't known, and the rest of the Navy adopted Vernon's drink as he made it. In time this was diluted further, and by the late nineteenth century grog was made with one part rum to four parts water and juice. The *Sailor's Word-Book* notes the existence of something even weaker called 'Six-water Grog', a further diluted version that was given as a punishment for drunkenness or neglect of duty.

An elaborate ritual for mixing and serving grog arose, with separate pipe tunes played for the handing of the keys to the rum locker to the bosun, for his arrival on deck with a guard of soldiers and a cask of rum, and for the moment when mixing was complete and the line of sailors could form. The rum was mixed with water in a half-barrel with a lid, called a 'scuttled

Doling out the rum ration in the British navy was a daily ceremony, and on special occasions the ration was doubled. This illustration from The Graphic shows sailors celebrating Queen Victoria's Jubilee in 1897.

butt' in the parlance of the day. Since plenty of gossip was exchanged while in the line to pick up the rum ration, the word 'scuttlebutt' evolved to describe idle conversation.

The most famous incident involving rum in the British Navy involved the death of Admiral Nelson, who was shot by a French sniper in the final moments of the Battle of Trafalgar. Rather than being buried at sea, his body was put in a cask of rum so it could be preserved for interment in England. On the way back, so many sailors tapped the cask that it was nearly empty except for the pickled admiral. The nickname 'Nelson's Blood' was adopted for Navy rum almost immediately, and is still widely used among sailors.

Grog continued to be drunk in the British Navy until 1970, by which time it had shed its disreputable character. A pivotal moment was when Queen Victoria reviewed the British fleet in March 1842: after drinking grog from the same tub as her common sailors, she earned their undying admiration by declaring that she liked it. The evidence of popular song suggests she was in the minority; of the sea shanties that have been conclusively dated to the age of sail, more express a longing for whiskey and beer than rum. One, 'Whiskey Johnny', takes a less discriminating attitude:

> The mate likes whiskey and the skipper likes rum,
> Whiskey! Johnny!
> The crew likes both, but we ain't got none,
> Whiskey for me Johnny!

The one that shows the most enthusiasm actually celebrates tapping a cargo:

> I wish I was Old Stormy's son,
> I'd build me a ship of a thousand ton,

> I'd fill yer up with Jamaica rum,
> And all the shellbacks they'd have some,

Another shanty that mentions rum, 'Sally Brown', has a West Indian beat and celebrates a local lady:

> Sally Brown's a bright mulatto,
> Way, hey, roll and go!
> She drinks rum and she chews tobacco,
> Going to spend my money on Sally Brown.

The final line suggests that Sally Brown's affection was negotiable, adding to the sense that she was anything but ladylike. For a sailor to be dreaming of a mixed-race prostitute who drinks rum and chews tobacco instead of a fair flower of English femininity was more than a little shocking for the era.

The romance of rum and the sea would be celebrated later, and romanticized during the Prohibition era in America, but it was economy and practicality that made it the beverage of choice in Britain's Atlantic and Caribbean trade in the eighteenth and nineteenth centuries.

As with merchant shipping, the Americans were warier of alcohol afloat. The US Navy served grog made with rum or whiskey from the earliest days of its existence until 1 September 1862. On 31 August of that year, the last day of the liquor ration, an officer named Caspar Schenk of the USS *Portsmouth* composed a ditty called 'Farewell to Grog'. It was sung to the tune of 'Landlord, Fill The Flowing Bowl', a merry song about rum punch, and ran in part,

> Come, messmates, pass the bottle 'round
> Our time is short, remember,

For our grog must stop,
And our spirits drop,
On the first day of September.

For tonight we'll merry, merry be,
For tonight we'll merry, merry be,
For tonight we'll merry, merry be,
Tomorrow we'll be sober.

Jack's happy days will soon be gone,
To return again, oh never!
For they've raised his pay five cents a day,
But stopped his grog forever.

The US Navy never did reinstate the grog tub, and did their best to block Caribbean rum runners during the US Civil War. Those shipments infuriated Confederate officials; most captains were British and interested only in profit, and they kept bringing in rum, silk and luxuries instead of desperately needed munitions. The British Caribbean had been in an economic downturn with the war raging to the north, so successful blockade runners could buy rum cheap and make huge profits. The end of the war brought little relief to the Caribbean planters and distillers, because though the country was at peace, the economy of the South was shattered and imports were a fraction of their previous volume.

4
Rum All over the World: Australia, India, Asia, South America and Beyond

Once you know that rum can be made from molasses, it really isn't very difficult to do it. Making good rum is another matter, one that involves redistilling and ageing, but it is fairly easy to make a strong, cheap alcoholic beverage. Wherever sugar was milled, rum distilling followed, and the profits to be made and portability of molasses meant that rum was made even in places where the hardiest cane could not thrive.

Rum and Rebellion in Nineteenth-century Australia

Sugar cane arrived in Australia with the first colonization fleet in 1787, and rum and whisky were made there as soon as the first stills arrived in 1793, but for a long time most rum was either imported or made with imported molasses. As was the case in British colonies in the Americas, there was a shortage of coinage and rum quickly became a de facto currency.

While Australia had few instances of seagoing piracy, the colony quickly developed a massive organized crime problem. The New South Wales Corps, the regiment of soldiers in charge of keeping order among convicts who were shipped to Australia, were as rough a crew as the prisoners they supervised. Australia was an unpopular posting, and the British Army had sent their worst troops to that continent, including some who were paroled from military prisons on condition that they go there. The New South Wales Corps quickly became known as the Rum Corps, and set a record for using their military connections to enrich themselves. The mark-up on the rum and whisky that they controlled was as much as 2,000 per cent, and illicit fortunes were made. Attempts by one governor to discipline an officer caught trading in illicit rum were complicated by the fact that all but one of his fellow officers were doing the same thing, so a jury of his peers could not be found. So much farmland was devoted to growing wheat for whisky and sugar for rum that there was a shortage of food even during a year of good harvests.

The previous governors having been ineffective at controlling the unruly troops, in 1805 the British government appointed someone who had an obvious genius at personnel management: Captain William Bligh. Bligh's first command had been the *Bounty*, which famously failed to reach its destination, and he was no more successful in his next – the crew of the Providence also mutinied. While on the way to Australia, Bligh and another captain, Joseph Short, quarrelled over the leadership of the fleet to the point where Short fired shots across the bow of Bligh's ship. Bligh responded by ordering his men to board Short's ship and arrest him. They did, and in that happy and convivial atmosphere Bligh arrived in Australia to discipline the Rum Corps.

The beginning of the Rum Rebellion of 1808 – this damaged watercolour from the period shows Govenor Bligh found hiding under his bed. The artist is said to be one of the mutineers.

Bligh proceeded to do sensible things in as abrasive a manner as possible. His actions included prohibiting officers from engaging in the illegal rum trade, and within a year a corps of officers deposed Bligh in an uprising called the Rum Rebellion. Bligh was overthrown and the head of the Rum Corps took his place, ceding it almost immediately to a newly arrived administrator named Joseph Foveaux. The Rum Corps officers may have thought Foveaux would be a pliable stooge, but the newcomer turned out to be the first effective, competent and politically savvy civilian administrator. The deposed Governor Bligh was held in genteel captivity throughout the year 1808, when he was granted a ship on the condition that he sail back to England. He immediately broke this promise and went to Tasmania instead to try to raise a force to take back his position. His instincts were as good as ever: the governor there refused to help and confined Bligh to his ship in the harbour for two years. The colonial overlords in London eventually came up with an interesting solution. Bligh went back to Sydney and symbolically governed for one day and then shipped out for London, shortly followed by the entire Rum Corps. New troops were rotated in, and the links between rum, the military and wholesale corruption was severed. Bligh was promoted to Rear Admiral but not given any ships to command, and finished his naval days without further incident. His career is immortalized in three brands of rum: Bounty brand rums are made in both Fiji and St Lucia, and Captain Bligh rum hails from St Vincent. Given the problems Bligh had with the *Bounty* and with rum in Australia, I have a feeling that he would not regard any of these as a compliment.

The first legal commercial rum production in Australia began in 1823, but was on a small scale until the 1860s, when vast tracts of sugar cane were planted in Queensland. The government did its best to regulate rum strictly and tax it heavily, inspiring one enterprising lawbreaker to an ingenious

Photo of the ss *Walrus*, the floating distillery designed to evade Australian customs inspectors, *c.* 1870.

solution: a floating cane crusher and distillery called the ss *Walrus*. A local character named James Stewart, alias 'Bosun Bill', took this paddlewheel steamer around the rivers of Queensland, easily evading inspectors while making an unknown and untaxed amount of rum. After a few years he quit the business and sold the boat's still to local entrepreneurs who started the Beenleigh Rum Distillery, which is still in operation. For many years they sold rum emblazoned with the smiling face of a man in a sailor's cap, known as Bosun Bill.

Rum in India and Asia

Eventually rum distilling returned to the place where making sugar from alcohol began. Charting the early history of rum in India is difficult, because so many beverages were carelessly referred to by the same name, arrack. This is now the name for distilled palm sugar, but as early as 1660 François Bernier recorded what he called an '*eau de vie de sucre*' made from unrefined sugar. This can hardly be anything other than rum, but we know nothing about it. It is often the case in societies where only aristocrats are literate that details of the merchant class are left to outsiders, who are often ill informed.

We do know that rum was widely made in colonial India, with the first industrial-level distillery opened by Carew & Co. in 1805 at Kanpur (Cawnpore) to supply the army. Before sugar was grown in Australia, that colony's needs were met by rum shipped from Calcutta, and the Navy depended on a ready supply for British outposts in Africa and Asia. Production grew steadily, though for decades local producers faced discriminatory tariffs that favoured sugar and rum from the West Indies. The high tariff did mean that much rum was

smuggled to neighbouring countries despite laws that prohibited the practice.

There were distinct differences between the rum made for the consumption of British troops and what was consumed locally. Rum distilled from sugar to international standards was usually called 'Indian made foreign liquor', or IMFL. 'Country rum' and 'arrack' were slang for locally produced alcoholic beverages made from anything that would ferment, often containing palm sugar, molasses and various flower essences.

The British believed that drinking rum warded off cholera, and in the 1820s Temperance-inclined soldiers could actually be punished for failing to drink their ration, but there were other tensions caused by religious beliefs. Muslim servants and orderlies in India sometimes objected to handling rum for the officers' mess, and many Hindus resented the British for introducing corrupting spirits into Indian society. When one prostitute was found plying her trade while actually living in a discarded rum barrel, it confirmed the worst nightmares of those who thought rum had a pernicious influence on society.

Rum was made on a smaller scale in Burma and other British Asian colonies, and some distilling was conducted in east and south Africa. Rum was made in Mauritius too, but in the eighteenth and nineteenth centuries it was of famously bad quality: in a parliamentary inquiry the Secretary for Foreign Affairs referred to it as 'inferior and poisonous'.

Rum came to Hawaii in the early nineteenth century, during the time that the British claimed the islands, and King Kamehameha I liked it so much that he ordered that it be

Three rums from Asia: Starr Rum from Mauritius, Mekhong 'Whisky' from Thailand and Old Monk from India.

made locally. The Hawaiians had traditionally made a kind of beer from the sweet roots of the *ti* plant, and when distilling equipment arrived on the islands they started experimenting both with making rum and with distilling their native liquor. The Hawaiians used old whaling pots that had an unusual shape, like Siamese twin cauldrons. They were made that way so they would fit inside ships' holds. The Hawaiians nicknamed those pots *okolehao*, or 'iron buttocks', and this came to be the generic name for liquors made from combinations of *ti* leaf, molasses and pineapple juice. The Hawaiians also made heavy, dark rum in those pots, which sold well to whaling crews and later became the signature flavour in Hawaiian cocktails.

Some island rulers didn't like rum as much as Kamehameha; after a look at the unruly effects of drunken sailors in Madagascar, the government of the time tried to ban its importation, despite pressure from the British. Prime Minister Rainilaiarivony memorably complained that the same boats that came loaded with missionaries and Bibles above decks were loaded with rum below, and while he was glad to welcome the foreigners he would not let in a single bottle of rum if he could help it. However, his protests were to no avail, and within a few years sugar was planted and rum distilled on his own island.

The only country in South Asia never conquered by the British or French was Thailand, where rum arrived with European traders in the sixteenth century. By 1830 Thais had developed distilled liquors called *lao khao*, literally 'white spirit', containing various mixtures of fermented sugar cane juice, molasses, rice and herbs. Quality control and standardization of their wares were literally alien concepts among Thai distillers, and no quality rum was made there until the twentieth century.

Rum in the Spanish and Portuguese Colonies during the Nineteenth Century

Meanwhile, back where rum began, the Brazilians continued making cachaça, but the improvement in quality was patchy and gradual. During the Napoleonic Wars when Portuguese monarchs ruled from exile in Rio de Janeiro, manufacture was prohibited, but it became legal again in 1821. In 1829 Dr Robert Walsh called it 'an inferior sort of rum so cheap and accessible that foreigners, particularly sailors, get greatly addicted to it'. He noted that 'A distiller has lately tried to improve it, and by a further process converted it into good rum.' Walsh was the first foreigner on record to say anything kind about cachaça, and Morewood noted a decade later that servants drank it with salt as a tonic, and it seemed to do them good. It was still a raw beverage, crudely made; while everyone else was using copper stills and ageing in wood, the Brazilians were using clay pots for both.

The most famous foreigner to write about Brazil in the nineteenth century, Sir Richard Francis Burton, had plenty of experience with cachaça, and hated it. In his book *The Highlands of Brazil* (1869) he described it as 'distilled from refuse molasses and drippings of clayed sugar', and said it tasted of 'copper and smoke, not Glenlivet'. He described two kinds: common, which was made from Cayenne cane, and *creoulinha* or *branquiunha*, made from Maideran cane. Of both, he said:

> Strangers are not readily accustomed to the odour, but a man who takes to it may reckon on delirium tremens and an early grave. Its legitimate use is for bathing after insolation, or for washing away the discomfort of insect bites.

Burton also used it to get his mastiff puppy drunk so it would stop snoring at night.

Burton was kinder about *restilo*, redistilled cachaça or *caninha*, jocularly called 'Brazilian wine', which he said did not have an unpleasant odour. (He referred to *restilo* as a molasses spirit only a sentence after referring to it as being made from cane juice; whether he was confused or Brazilians were actually distilling both is difficult to determine.) Burton used *restilo* to preserve the snakes he captured in his expedition, though he noted that the alcohol affected the colour of the specimens. Mention was made of a triple-distilled version called *lavado*, or washed, which was said to be

A traditional copper alembic still in use at Cachaça Leblon in Brazil.

so pure that if it were tossed in the air, much of it would evaporate before it came down.

Burton also recorded two related slang terms: *cachaçada*, literally meaning 'what happens when you drink cachaça' – in other words, a drunken fight – and *pinga*, a slang term for rum that literally means 'the drip'. This image, of alcohol dripping from a crude still of the type everyone else had long ago abandoned, is probably the best indication of how far the Brazilians had to go to catch up with the rest of the world.

Among the Spanish colonies Cuba had the ideal weather and soil for sugar, but restrictive laws and the stifling Spanish bureaucracy kept it an economic backwater. Cuban rum was famously murky and stinking until an enterprising wine merchant named Facundo Bacardi became interested in making it better. After considerable experimentation with charcoal filtering and oak barrel ageing, he managed to make a pure, clear spirit that was unlike any Cuban rum produced before, and he released it to the public in 1862. Having been a merchant, Bacardi understood the power of branding, and he claimed to have drawn from Taino lore to develop the bat symbol that is the best-known trademark in the industry. In a well-run entrepreneurial society, Bacardi would have prospered in peace, but the Spanish Empire's last major Caribbean colony was on the brink of collapse. Slave revolts (the institution was not abolished until 1886), trade embargoes and other upheavals kept the business precarious for three decades, and Facundo's first rum-producing company went bankrupt. His son and successor Emilio was repeatedly jailed under suspicion of supporting the rebels, and the company survived only due to his dedication. It was not until the close of the Spanish–American war in 1898 that Bacardi was able to settle down to making rum unhindered by politics, and when it did it made up for lost time.

'Rum' that Wasn't Rum

The nineteenth century saw the invention of two items that weren't actually rum as we know it – '*inlander* rum', as exemplified by Stroh's of Austria, and bay rum. Inlander rum was a response to the popularity of rum drinks in countries that had no tropical colonies, and hence no sugar. It was invented in about 1820 by a pharmacist in the Austrian city of Krems, who used a mix of grain alcohol, caramel made from beet

Distilleries were often built like fortresses due to concerns about revolts by the workers. This picture of Rummerie St James in the Netherlands Antilles is an example.

Bottle of Bay Rum hair dressing from the 1950s. No matter how thirsty you are, do not drink this.

sugar and herbs to mimic the taste of rum. In 1832 Sebastian Stroh started brewing his version of this concoction in Klagenfurt, and he quickly became the dominant producer. Inlander rum became an integral part of hot toddies made with rum and tea, and was also used in a flaming cocktail called *Feuerzangenbowle*. This cocktail has an elaborate presentation: a sugar cube is soaked with inlander rum and set on fire so that the molten sugar drips into hot mulled wine. Making *Feuerzangenbowle* – literally, fire-tongs bowl – is still a tradition among German college fraternities, but since 1995 the rum in it has been made with molasses. Stroh's and other companies still flavour their rum so it tastes like their original recipe, a rare case of a product that mimics a counterfeit of itself.

Nobody is going to counterfeit the taste of bay rum, because it is not designed for drinking. Bay rum comes from the island of St John in the Caribbean, but it is an aftershave and deodorant made from rosemary and the leaves of the bay laurel tree soaked in rum. It smells nice but tastes horrible, and it was once regarded a hilarious practical joke at colleges to serve a neophyte drinker bay rum and watch them gag. It deserves a mention here only so that nobody who reads this book will fall for that trick.

Rum, Wars and Exploration

Once the British adopted the practice of rum rations for the Navy, the other services were quick to follow. Though the blockade of France during the Napoleonic Wars never entirely shut off the flow of wine and brandy from the Continent, dependence on smuggled supplies for military rations was obviously a bad idea. Rum caught on quickly, and became so much a part of British military life that one chronicler literally suggested that it had magical powers. Sita Ram, an officer who began his career in the Bengal Army of East India in 1812, wrote in his autobiography that

> I am sure there is some elixir of life in ration rum; I have seen wounded men, all but dead, come to life after having some rum given to them. Be this as it may, I am convinced there is something very extraordinary about it. I know European soldiers worship liquor, give their lives for it, and often lose their lives trying to get it.

Each enlisted man was entitled to a third of a pint (*c.* 200 ml) of rum per day, and that dependable supply of liquor was necessary for morale. As the Duke of Wellington put it, 'People talk of their enlisting from their fine military feeling – all stuff – no such thing. Some of our men enlist from having got bastard children – some for minor offences – many more for drink.' Soldiers also received a ration of tobacco, which like rum was regarded as a health food. A contemporary account of the Peninsular War by a serving officer includes this poem, in which a regimental doctor gives his patient a prescription that modern physicians are unlikely to endorse:

'Come', says the doctor 'here is rum and segars –
This is the way we carry on our wars.
Here, smoke, my boy, I know 'twill do you good;
And try this country wine, 'twill cool your blood.'

If this was an exaggeration, it wasn't much of one. After campaigning in Ceylon in 1805, Captain Robert Percival of the Royal Irish Regiment wrote:

In this 1798 etching by Johann Ramberg, an officer has tossed his sword beside an empty rum cask and is flirting with local women, while his troops carouse in the background. Only the stray dogs seem interested in fighting.

Drinking plenty of Arrack and smoking tobacco counteract the bad effects of the atmosphere and the water, while the natives on the other hand live so abstemiously, few or none of them eating flesh or drinking anything but water, that once they are seized with the exhausting distempers they want strength to resist them and they usually fall victims.

Percival and his men drank imported West Indian rum when they could, but sometimes had to buy inferior rum that was made locally by Dutch entrepreneurs.

It was not unusual for officers to supply rum from local manufacturers when rations were low, and this was often bought from their own wages. Requests for reimbursement

The idea that rum is a healthy beverage lasted a long time. This German-language poster for Coruba Rum of Jamaica boasts that it helps you to warm up, 1930s.

arrived in London along with complaints about how bad and expensive local rum usually was. Sometimes this rum was even poisonous, as in the case of the entire garrison on the island of Marie-Galante that was laid low by rum made in a crude still with soldered lead pipes. One positive effect of the mass consumption of alcohol by British soldiers was that government quartermasters made the first tentative steps toward regulating its quality and strength.

Another ramification of the Napoleonic Wars had long-range consequences for tropical sugar production. Since the French were cut off from their Caribbean sources for sugar they sought substitutes, and in 1812 Benjamin Delessert devised the first commercially practical method of extracting sugar from sugar beet. The availability of sugar from a crop that could be grown in Europe, and hence had low transport costs to major markets, meant that Caribbean sugar had competition for the first time. By 1855 the world-wide price of sugar slumped due to overproduction and the competition from beet sugar. Beet sugar was useless for making rum due to sulphuric by-products that imparted a strong flavour to the liquor when distilled, and cane sugar producers soon realized that rum would be an increasingly important source of income.

Among the most successful at improving the quality of their rum were planters in what is now the nation of Guyana. Demerara rum was regarded as poor at the outbreak of the Napoleonic Wars, but a consortium of distillers hired experts to improve it. Their precise contributions are not well documented and may just have involved enforcing cleanliness in the production facilities, but it is certain that the quality improved greatly. Interest in the colony and its produce was heightened by a book published in 1813 titled *A Voyage To The Demerary*. The author, Henry Bolingbroke, rhapsodized about the idyllic nature of the area, the quality of its sugar and its boundless commercial opportunities. Bolingbroke insisted that slaves in Guyana were better treated and happier with their lot than sailors in the British Navy. The accuracy of his impression that these slaves were cheerful and contented may be judged against the fact that they revolted en masse just over a decade later, but his assessment of the sugar and rum were accurate.

Demerara rum was advertised as an effective remedy for cold and chills. The packaging shows the casual racism that celebrated African slaves working in British South American colonies.

In 1838 Morewood noted that

the superior quality of the rum manufactured in the colony of Demerary has, it is thought, injured the demand for the rum of the islands. Its distillation . . . has been carried to a high state of perfection by the persever-ance and skill of several scientific men, who have succeeded in causing the rum of Essequibo and Demer-rary to be as much in request in the American market as that of Jamaica is in England.

The American Civil War disrupted that trade, but even after the conflict was over, rum sales to the USA declined. The Temperance movement was gaining adherents, and cities and towns were experimenting with banning or severely restricting the sale of alcohol.

5
Rum Falls from Grace and Rises Again: Temperance, Cocktails, Wars and Religion

The original Temperance movement began in Britain around 1800, and advocated not the abolition of alcohol, but temperate – or moderate – imbibing. As time went on the movement in America became more radical, and began agitating for a ban on the sale of all alcohol. In June 1851 the movement notched up its first success and its first public relations disaster in quick succession when the state of Maine outlawed the sale of alcohol except for medical and industrial purposes. The law was spearheaded by Mayor Neal S. Dow of Portland, who styled himself the 'Napoleon of Temperance'. Within four years ten other states and numerous cities and counties had gone dry, and Dow looked poised for a place in national politics. His career stalled when a search warrant was issued for a shipment of liquor that he personally had arranged. Though there was little doubt that this alcohol actually was for medicinal purposes as he had claimed, an angry mob denounced him as a hypocrite and started throwing rocks at his property. This marked the beginning of what came to be called the Portland Rum Riot, which ended when the militia fired on a crowd, killing one man and wounding seven others. The conflict damaged the Temperance movement in Maine, and the law was repealed in 1856. Dow went on to become a Union general, the founder of the National Temperance Society and Publishing House, and the Prohibitionist Party's candidate for President.

By the end of Dow's career he was widely regarded as a cranky buffoon, but the movement he championed was a force in culture as well as politics. New towns such as Greeley, Colorado, and Temperance, Ohio, were founded with charters that banned alcohol in perpetuity, and Republican-leaning newspapers printed lyrics to Temperance songs in their pages. Many of these rail against rum, possibly because there are more potential rhymes for it than whiskey, which was actually more popular at the time. A typical example, 'Father's a Drunkard and Mother is Dead', printed in the *Baltimore Sun* about 1870, includes these deathless lines:

> We were all happy, till father drank rum,
> Then all our sorrow and trouble begun,
> Mother grew paler and wept every day,
> Baby and I were too hungry to play.
> Slowly they faded, on one summer night,
> I found their sweet faces both silent and white.
> With the big tears slowly dropping, I said,
> Father's a drunkard and mother is dead.

There are several recordings of this song from the Edison Cylinder days, and the tune is surprisingly sprightly. The same can not be said of 'Lips That Touch Liquor Shall Never Touch Mine', a song so popular that it spawned at least two sets of lyrics: one a surprisingly well-written tale of a temperate maid rejecting a drunken suitor, and the other a call to arms for anti-alcohol actions. The latter captures the flavour of the militant Temperance footsoldiers very well:

Let war be your watchword, from shore unto shore,
Till Rum and his legions shall ruin no more,
And write on your banners, in letters that shine,
The lips that touch liquor shall never touch mine.

'Demon rum' was the shorthand for all manner of liquor, and those who abused alcohol became known as 'rummies'.

Temperance hit the headlines in 1835 when a Massachusetts minister named George Cheever published a poem called 'Deacon Giles' Distillery', an account of a man who was a minister at weekends, but made his living distilling rum. In the story demons ran the distillery after the workers went home and manufactured all the evils of the world. Everyone in Salem recognized it as a caricature of John Stone, a Unitarian minister who did in fact own a distillery. Mobs supporting Stone attacked the publisher, and Cheever was jailed for libel. Cheever became a national Temperance leader and his poem was widely circulated with inventive and lurid images.

Temperance forces were quick to link rum with Satan, as in this image of devils operating a distillery from 1835.

Rum was also used in the generic sense in a famous slogan that doomed the 1884 presidential candidacy of James G. Blaine. A minister who was speaking at a campaign event for Blaine thundered that opposition candidate Grover Cleveland's Southern and Catholic support made his Democrats the party of 'Rum, Romanism, and Rebellion'. Blaine, who was present, ignored the remark and thought it was unimportant, but the national audience that read about it in the newspapers found it too intolerant. Public opinion turned against him, and he was the only non-incumbent Republican to lose a Presidential election between 1860 and 1912. It was a setback for a movement that was to have its moment of triumph and failure after the dawn of a new century.

The Early Twentieth Century: Rum Runners and Tiki Bars

The sale of alcoholic beverages was banned in the early years of the twentieth century in the Soviet Union, Hungary, Iceland, Norway, Finland, several Canadian provinces and the Australian Capital Territory of Canberra. Most of these laws had already been recognized as failures and repealed when the USA embarked on the utopian social experiment of Prohibition in 1920. It had been a long time coming; the legislation to enact it had been proposed in 1917, and private citizens had had plenty of time to stock up on booze. Organized crime had had plenty of time to prepare, too, and they were far more ready than the police for what was to come.

Since the word 'rum' was already shorthand for all forms of liquor, the press quickly coined a new vocabulary of compound words. Entrepreneurs who smuggled contraband in small boats were called rum runners even if their cargo was

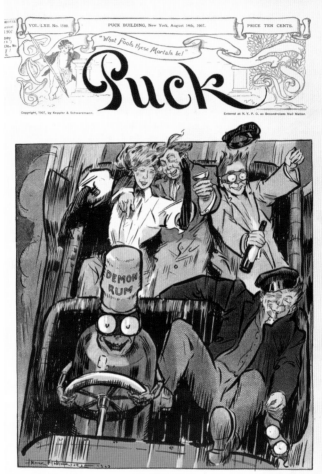

ONE PHASE OF IT.

Driving while drunk was recognized as a social problem as early as 1907, when *Puck* arrtist Frank Nankivell put Demon Rum at the wheel of a speeding car.

whiskey and gin, and the large vessels that floated just out-side the three-mile limit were called rum sows. Fleets of smuggling ships were referred to as the rum fleet or rum row, and the ships that preyed on them and stole their cargo were quite logically called rum pirates. In 1927 Supreme Court Chief Justice William Howard Taft invented another phrase that didn't catch on when he referred to a ship as 'hovering with rumful purpose'.

A large percentage of the public sympathized with these men and romanticized the smuggler's life, and that of other lawbreakers who set up alcohol distribution networks. It was recognized even then that Prohibition was the greatest gift to organized crime in American history, and ardent Prohibitionists were widely depicted in popular culture as busybodies and prigs. One such portrayal in popular culture showed Prohibitionists in terms as apocalyptic as the ones they used for alcoholics. The 1927 play *Spellbound*, according to a review in *Life* magazine,

> expounds the curse of cursing drink. It holds up the horrible example of a mother so intent upon defeating Demon Rum that she flushes her two little sons with anti-whiskey solutions. The result: one becomes a mute, the other a paralytic. Later in life, a thunderstorm suddenly starts up during the third act to provide atmosphere while the mute is engaged in raping a girl. This reprehensible sight so enrages the paralytic that he suddenly renews his synaptic connections, skips out of bed, does successful battle for the Right.

The review noted that 'The play's existence testifies to at least one of the evils of Prohibition.'

Prohibitionists were often decried as hypocrites, and the public was delighted whenever a prominent one was caught red-handed. In 1929 Congressman M. Alfred Michaelson was allowed 'free entry' for ponderous baggage which, on investigation, was found to contain kegged gallons of rum and bottled quarts of strong liquors. Michaelson's explanation that his brother-in-law Walter Gramm had packed his bags for him was met with some scepticism, but the case was eventually dropped and Gramm paid a fine of $1,000.

Officials were even ridiculed when they were caught eating things made with rum rather than drinking it. General Lincoln Andrews, returning from a conference with the British on smuggling prevention, was spotted in the dining salon of the liner *La France* eating crêpes with rum sauce. When challenged, he replied that 'everything eaten with a fork or a spoon was quite all right'. Andrews called his meeting with the British '125% successful'. If anyone asked him about the irony that the British Navy ships were supposed to stop rum smuggling while serving daily rum rations to their own sailors, his reply has been lost.

Business on cruise ships like the *La France* that continued to serve liquor boomed, as did tourism to the Caribbean islands that welcomed drinkers. The losers, of course, were those American possessions that complied with the law. The tally of cruise ship calls at St Thomas dropped from 90 per month to 25, and the value of the island's exports, which were limited almost exclusively to rum, fell from $3,571,787 in 1921, to $754,729 in 1922.

Those vacation destinations that didn't enforce Prohibition reaped the benefits, and increased tourism and rum sales were all the more important because of the crash in commodity prices: sugar that cost over 20 cents a pound in 1920 fetched 3 cents a pound in 1921. All rum-producing islands in the Caribbean made their pitch for American tourists, none so successfully as Cuba. Writers like Ernest Hemingway popularized exotic drinks like the Daiquiri, Mojito and Cuba libre, and the Bacardi Company ran ads that proclaimed, 'Come to Cuba and bathe in Bacardi rum!' Movie stars trekked from Hollywood and New York to Havana, and the Floridita and other nightclubs became famous for style and decadence. Other islands benefited as well: Haiti was going through a rare period of peace and good governance and reaped considerable benefits, and Bermuda capitalized on the inflow of liquor from both Europe and the Caribbean to become the world capital of liquor smuggling.

While governments of Caribbean countries and officials of European navies routinely agreed to assist the us Navy and Customs Service in combating smuggling, it is hard to believe that they were trying very hard. Countries that profited from the smuggling trade obviously had no great interest in putting a stop to it, and found America's spasm of righteousness more than a little ridiculous. Americans eventually agreed,

Sloppy Joe's in Havana was the most famous bar in the western hemisphere during Prohibition. A later establishment of the same name in Key West copied its style and drinks. The picture is of the Havana location in the early 1930s.

and the legislation to repeal the act passed in 1933 and went into effect in 1935.

Prohibition had a massive effect on America's native liquor industry, wiping out all but a few of the remaining New England distilleries. It also signalled a major change in American tastes. As *Life* magazine put it in December 1933,

> The pre-War liquor business was the whiskey business. In 1913 the US drank 135,000,000 gal. of rye and Bourbon, 5,000,000 gallons of gin, 1,500,000 gallons of Scotch, a trickle of Irish. Rum, wine, brandy, liqueurs cut no figure . . . That in 1934 the US will drink at least 200,000,000 gallons of something seems certain.

Though the article suggested that whiskey would likely regain its former prominence, it noted that 'Bacardi rum is more widely known in the US today than ever it was before Prohibition.'

Since the few American distilleries that remained in business would take some time to restart operations and age their product, foreign liquor had the American market to itself for some time afterward. Even before the repeal was officially in effect, Sloppy Joe's in Key West became famous for the Mojito cocktails that regular customer Ernest Hemingway enjoyed so much, and in Los Angeles a bartender named Ernest Gantt opened a bar called Don the Beachcomber and introduced a rum drink called the Zombie. Gantt invented not only the drink that is one of the most powerful tipples in a bartender's arsenal, but the concept of the Polynesian-themed tiki bar, and he eventually changed his name to Donn Beach to capitalize on the name of his famous bar. Gantt's customers included Charlie Chaplin, Howard Hughes and other Hollywood celebrities, who were happy to try his other

Don the Beachcomber, the man who made tropical drinks famous, in his natural element.

creations, such as Tahitian punch and his version of Navy grog. Gantt was a canny businessman who understood the psychology of his customers. Behind the bar he had a tap for a garden hose mounted on the roof, and he would turn it on when the bar was full, so customers would think it was raining and would stay until the shower was over.

Gantt's success inspired San Francisco native Vic Bergeron to start his own restaurant, Trader Vic's, with his own rum drink, the Mai Tai (named after the Tahitian word for 'good'). Both establishments spawned dozens of imitators

The tropical allure of rum and remote islands – label from a bottle of Man Friday rum, 1940.

and became chains, and the tiki bar phenomenon spread across America. People in the American heartland who had never even seen the Pacific ate bad Chinese food while sipping rum drinks out of fake coconuts and dreaming of tropical breezes. It was a marketing work of genius, and established an image for rum that still endures.

World War, World Rum and Today

While America was repealing Prohibition, a bizarre incident in London put rum in the European headlines. For over a century a set of docks and warehouses on the Thames had been known as Rum Quay, and over three million litres of liquor were stored there in 6,500 wooden barrels. On 21 April 1933 a small fire at a neighbouring lumberyard spread to the warehouse, and the entire stock ignited. The burning rum spread over half the width of the river and burned for four days, and firemen trying to fight the blaze were made tipsy by the fumes. The amount lost was almost equal to the entire annual production of Barbados at that time and, along with the surging demand from America, caused a spike in rum prices.

Nicaragua, which produces some excellent rums, probably had some extra product available to put on the market in the autumn of that year. In a break with tradition, President Carlos Jarquín ordered that none of the parties were to provide voters with free rum at polling places. It is hard to tell whether turnout that year was so low because of this or because the election had obviously been rigged by the military, but rum was given away at the next election.

The Second World War interrupted the rum trade again, and in many places distilleries were assigned to make industrial alcohol of the type used to fuel torpedoes. (It was poisonous, but soldiers and sailors figured out ways to purify it and drank it anyway.) In the Philippines, which had begun producing rum on a grand scale in the late nineteenth century, this alcohol was regarded as a munition, and as the Japanese advanced toward Manila the government pleaded with distillers to dump their entire stock of rum. Most did, and the Japanese imprisoned the owners of the distilleries as a consequence.

Places where people were accustomed to imported alcohol but couldn't get it started making their own, as in Uganda, where local sugar and palm spirit was distilled into *waragi*, the local pronunciation of 'war gin'. In Thailand in 1941, with most export markets closed, an expatriate brewer named James Honzatko took advantage of the low price of

The first Asian brands of rum sold in American market had little success. Rocroy was only briefly available in the USA, and it is a fair bet that when this ad appeared in 1948 most people had never heard of Réunion Island, where it was made.

sugar by brewing a concoction he called Mekong whiskey. Actually a rum made of 95 per cent molasses and 5 per cent rice and herbs, it became the national spirit of Thailand and was distributed all over Southeast Asia after the war.

Meanwhile, traditional rum producers in the Caribbean and South America were devastated by closed markets in Continental Europe, vastly increased shipping rates, and loss of cargoes to U-boat warfare. There were of course local sales to American soldiers who had bases in the islands, which caused social friction because of the wealth of the GIs compared to the locals. This was commemorated in a song made famous by the Andrews Sisters, who were given the lyrics the night before the session and hadn't yet realized they were singing about prostitution:

From Chicachicaree to Mona's Isle
Native girls all dance and smile
Help soldier celebrate his leave
Make every day like New Year's Eve
Drinkin' rum and Coca-Cola
Go down Point Koomahnah
Both mother and daughter
Workin' for the Yankee dollar.

The song had been written by a pair of Trinidadian musicians and plagiarized by Morey Amsterdam, who obscured the meaning slightly – the original included lyrics about a newly-wed wife who ran away with an American soldier. Most people paid no more attention to the lyrics than the Andrews Sisters had, hearing only the chorus and dreaming of rum drinks and accommodating native women in a tropical paradise.

After the war's end many former colonies achieved independence and began marketing their rum outside traditional

Most ads for rum show black and brown people making rum and white people drinking it. This ad from a Havana newspaper in the 1950s was aimed at a local audience; the text reads, 'The beauty of Cuban women is unique in the world – the same is true of Matusalem.'

channels. Some became market leaders. Though most Americans have never heard of Old Monk rum from India, as of this writing it is the third best-selling rum in the world. Meanwhile, companies like Bacardi of Cuba expanded their operations and became true multinationals, making rum in several different countries. The head of the company in the 1950s, Pepin Bosch, had been expanding capacity outside Cuba for years, and their facility in Mexico was the largest distillery in the world. When Castro took over Cuba and nationalized the company, Bacardi was hardly affected, especially since they had recently shipped huge orders from Cuba to buyers all over the Caribbean, who hadn't yet paid for it. The deliveries were planned by Bosch, who spirited his spirits away from the Communist regime and left the island with his family just in time. Bacardi shifted their headquarters to Puerto Rico and continued selling rum without a single missed delivery. Bacardi continues to assert its heritage and annoy the Cuban government by producing rum under the name Havana Club, which is also trademarked by a government-owned Cuban distillery. While legal battles rage over the name, the Cuban version of Havana Club is sold almost everywhere except the USA.

Rum took a back seat to vodka, gin and other spirits in the 1960s and '70s, but has made a resurgence in popularity since then. New players entered the international market, and in 1990 – only 400 years after it was invented, give or take a few decades – the Brazilians finally marketed cachaça outside their own country. Rums and *aguardientes* from other parts of South America became prominent later in the decade, and Zacapa rum from Guatemala became the first Central American spirit to top international competitions.

A decade into the twenty-first century, rum is being made all over the world by both traditional and inventive methods, and brands that were unheard of only a decade ago are selling for premium prices. Speciality rum bars cater to an increasingly knowledgeable crowd, and rums are savoured with the attention usually given to fine brandy and Scotch whisky. It

THE CARIBBEAN HAS NEVER SEEN A PIRATE LIKE FIDEL.
HE STOLE AN ISLAND AND THREW THE TREASURE AWAY.

Matusalem

EXPELLED FROM CUBA IN 1959

Bacardi was the famous name in Cuban rum, but another company had
the best ads. This caricature of Fidel Castro as a peg-legged pirate was an
ad for the Matusalem Rum Company, which moved to the Dominican
Republic after the Communist takeover of Cuba.

has been an amazing change in status for a drink made from
what was once regarded as industrial waste, fit only for slaves
who could hope for no better antidote to their cares. A little
later I'll address the future of rum, but first it's worth looking at some of the ways in which rum has become entwined
in culture and religion.

Voodoo and Other Rituals of Rum

Rum has been a part of so many cultures for so long that rituals and traditions have grown up around it. Voodoo is the most
famous, but rum is also a ritual beverage in Cuban Santería
and Brazilian Quimbanda cults. All are based on African reli-
gions as modified in the New World, but the spirits are seen as
benevolent in some traditions, bloodthirsty in others.

Voodoo is based on rituals from Benin and is practised in Louisiana and Haiti, though the rituals in each place are markedly different. Both share the concept that there are powerful spirits called *loas* that can be invoked by the promise of sensory experiences in this world. The supplicant enters a trance state and invites the spirits to enter their body, and while there to enjoy earthly pleasures. These include food, drinking, tobacco and sexual intercourse, and each spirit has their favourite combination – for instance, the love goddess Erzulie appreciates offerings of fried pork, rum and cigarettes. Baron Samedi, the *loa* who is the guardian of the underworld, prefers cigars with his rum, and Haitian believers are certain that any offering other than Barbancourt premium rum will not merit his attention.

Voodoo rituals can involve drunken sex, and the worshipper often claims not to remember the actions of their body while it was possessed by the spirits. At the end of the trance state they are given a message from the spirits, usually

Bottles of rum are lined up as gifts to the spirits at this voodoo rite in Benin.

a prophecy or promise to intercede in the worshipper's favour. The *loas* are capricious and greedy, and often cloak their promises in ambiguous language worthy of a Greek oracle.

Voodoo worshippers keep altars in their homes, and start most ceremonies by pouring rum on the altar to get the *loas'* attention. Both Haitian and Louisiana voodoo rituals involve intricate drumming, but the Haitian ceremonies are more structured and closer to the African roots, the Louisiana more freeform.

Santería is a Cuban offshoot of Nigerian Yoruba tradition that was shaped by the necessity of the worshippers to hide their beliefs from the Spanish Inquisition. The *loas* are associated with Catholic saints who are venerated with extreme fervour using rituals seen nowhere else in the Christian world. The religion was long considered a mere cover for pagan traditions, but after the Spanish fell from power, Santería worshippers did not revert to their African beliefs – they continued baptizing their children and offering the saints gifts of rum, cigars and sugar. Priests called Santeros also offer animal sacrifices, first chanting and drumming so that any evil influences that plague a supplicant are drawn into a dove or chicken, then killing the bird so that the evil is dispersed. Santeros insist that their practices are different from black magic or witchcraft, and that they will only be a force for good.

Quimbanda makes no such claims. Followers of this Brazilian cult worship Exu, the god of chaos and trickery, or Ogu, god or war and metal. The rituals are explicitly designed to obtain power and revenge, and typically involve lighting seven candles and seven cigarettes, opening seven bottles of cachaça, and sacrificing an animal. Quimbanda is explicitly black magic, and has a more gentle and spiritual counterpart called Umbanda that has some resemblance to Santería. According to some authorities, cachaça is more important in

Quimbanda since it draws and compels the wilder and more malevolent spirits. There are many variants of Afro-Brazilian spirit worship, but in all of them cachaça is regarded as having unique power to call up spirits.

Strangely, rum has similar potency in a religious tradition with no African roots, that of the highland natives of Chiapas, Mexico. The Tzotzil Maya people in this area have a long tradition of giving offerings to the water spirits, and at some time – nobody knows exactly when – it was decided that the most effective gifts were bottles of rum and Coca-Cola. Some Tzotzil practice a hybrid religion like Santería in which Christian and native ideas are entwined, and Catholic priests in the area are used to offerings of rum to the saints.

Rum has also evolved one secular ritual, equivalent to the salt and lime tasting of tequila. This involves aged dark rum, limes, brown sugar and instant coffee. One is expected to dip one side of the lime into the sugar, the other side into the coffee, then suck on the lime, then taste the rum. The Pampero company of Venezuela decided to advertise this ritual in Italy with the slogan 'Il rum piu bevuto nei peggiori bar di Caracas' ('The rum most drunk in the worst bar in Caracas'). Strangely, it was a hit, and both Pampero rum and its tasting ritual are now popular in Europe.

6
Rum Today and Tomorrow

A book could be written just about the different types of stills used to produce rum and how various ageing techniques affect the final product: in fact, at least one has been. The engineering is interesting but not essential to know in order to appreciate rum. That said, it is worth considering how the raw materials, distilling equipment and ageing techniques have always shaped the final product.

Cane rums have a distinctive vegetable flavour to them, which can be an advantage or a liability depending on how highly refined the alcohol is and how it is aged. In crudely refined and unaged cane rums that character is unpleasant, but it is an advantage when this rum is aged in wood – the vegetable flavour mellows into a rich undertone.

Molasses rums begin with a sweeter, more concentrated sugar product that often has smoky or burnt flavours from the refining process. Depending on how highly the molasses is refined and how completely it is distilled, the resulting liquor can range from heavy and oily to thin and sharp-tasting.

Rum is made in two different types of stills: the alembic or pot stills that were used by medieval alchemists and the column still. Column stills were invented in 1830 and are far more efficient, but remove more flavours from the resulting

A field worker delivers sugar cane to the mill by bicycle in Mauritius.

alcohol. Pot still rums tend to have a sharper, smokier flavour, equivalent to the peaty Highland Scotch whiskies, while column-still rums are smoother, like Lowland whiskies. Most rum is distilled multiple times and filtered to remove impurities before being either sold unaged or barrel-aged to add smoothness and character. There is no consensus on how long rums should be aged for, and some are in the wood as little as one year, some for over twenty. As might be expected, the longer rums are aged the more their flavours become mellow and akin to aged whiskies. The different molasses and cane flavours are lost over time and the flavours converge; very old rum tastes much more like other rums of the same age than like its younger counterpart.

The type of wood used in ageing also makes a difference, and political changes have occasionally forced shifts in materials. Bourbon distilleries in America use their charred oak barrels once and then sell them, and Caribbean rum producers found that reusing these produced particularly mellow rum. When Prohibition came into effect the supply was cut off, and rum producers had to shift to used wine barrels from Europe, which cost more and didn't produce as desirable a product. The supply didn't resume immediately at the end of Prohibition in the USA, because the legal whiskey industry was at a standstill, and it was years before more American barrels were back on the market.

Spiced and fruited rums have a long heritage dating back to the days when most rum was so bad that it was almost undrinkable without some alteration. Spiced rums were also concocted by pharmacists as tonics, and in time they gained a following for beverages that tasted more of tropical herbs than molasses, cane and wood. In the last decade, premium spiced rums such as The Kraken have shown that it is possible to create a multi-dimensional drink in which the flavour of quality rum shows through. The genre seems to be headed for greater respectability, but rum purists will probably never really warm to it.

The same is true of fruit-infused rums, which are almost invariably bland and sugary confections. Most fruited rums are rightly classed as alcopops, and best left to the unsophisticated and underage drinkers that are their intended market. They are a boon to bartenders who value speed rather than quality. Real fruit juice and decent rum is a justly celebrated combination, and the small amount of time it takes to mix your own is worth it.

How Experts Enjoy Rum

It is hard to find any meaningful data about how people drink their rum worldwide, but it's safe to say that at least 90 per cent is blended with some kind of fruit juice or other flavouring. These drinks are usually served over ice, which further masks the subtle differences in taste and scent of the spirit.

Straight rum has not historically been served with any thought about how to enhance its flavour. It still isn't: if you order rum neat at most bars it will be served at an inappropriate temperature using the wrong glassware. Shot and cordial glasses do nothing to focus the aromas toward your nose so that you catch subtleties, and the best you can do in a typical place is to ask for it to be served in a wineglass.

I have read an expert's opinion that rum is best tasted at temperatures between 53 and 57 °F (12–14 °C), and best drunk from a balloon snifter or a sherry glass called a *copita*. To which I say: well, maybe. The wide range of flavour in modern rums extends from the almost vodka-like clarity and crispness of Treaty Oak Rum (Texas) to the rich, full sweetness of Old

Monk (India), butterscotch and caramel of Zacapa (Guatemala), and peppery exuberance of Sang Som (Thailand). Such different drinks may well warrant different glassware and temperatures. That said, snifters can concentrate the evaporating alcohol to the point where other scents are overwhelmed, so

David Morrison, Senior Blender for Appleton Rums of Jamaica, displays his wares at a rum tasting dinner in Los Angeles.

only the oldest and most full-flavoured rums ought to be drunk this way.

If you enjoy the vanilla and caramel scents of aged rums, you may prefer them a few degrees warmer than is usually considered optimal, and your glassware of choice is likely to be a snifter. As with Scotch whisky, a few drops of water – no more – can be surprisingly effective at opening up the flavours. Those who like white rums neat tend to like them cool but not cold, and often use a white wine glass or brandy-tasting glass.

The most interesting comment I got from interviewing several bartenders who specialize in rum was from John Colthorp of Caña in Los Angeles. He noted that you can accent different characteristics of rums using different glassware, but at the cost of learning less about it.

> Professionals taste using an iso tasting glass at room temperature, and if you really want to get a sense of the character of the rum, you'll taste them all in the same type of glass without correcting for the style. I drink it at room temperature, and don't understand why people drink it chilled – it reduces evaporation and dulls the nose, and why would you want that? As for water, it does help you notice fruitier aspects, and some people like it. As the rum changes proof, you open up different flavors.

As with everything else in food and beverages, the important thing is what you like, so if you discover you like your rum out of a coffee mug or straight from a hip flask, it's your business. Try it the expert's way some time, just to see if you're missing something, but enjoy it in whatever way makes you happiest.

Rum Cocktails

Anyone who tries to recreate early rum drinks is faced with an unusual problem: the worst rum you can buy now is better than the best rum in the world then. Other ingredients have changed too: culinary historians argue over whether the lemons called for in early recipes should be replaced by limes, and how to approximate the flavours of long-lost cultivars of Seville oranges and wild coconuts. Even those few recipes that include proportions can be problematic: what does 'the juice of five lemons' mean when the lemons we have to work with now have been bred for hundreds of years to yield lots of sweet juice? The best we can do is make educated guesses and experiment with enthusiasm, which is what the people who created these recipes did in the first place.

Early rum was so raw and unpalatable that even slaves seeking mere oblivion were creative about adding something to kill the taste and mute the harsh sharpness of the alcohol. Cachaça was mixed with cane and fruit juice in Brazil, and Morewood recorded that slaves on the plantations were given a beverage called 'weak diversion' made from rum, water and molasses. We don't know the exact proportions, and even if we did, it is unlikely to be a diverting experience.

The trinity of rum, citrus and sugar makes its appearance very early; Bacardi traces the drink's roots back to one of Sir Francis Drake's captains in 1586. That dating may be fanciful, but it certainly wasn't long after that before something very much like a Mojito was being sipped cautiously around the Caribbean. Lemons and limes were brought by Columbus on his second voyage in 1493, so when sugar and rum made their appearance, all the ingredients were available.

Rum punch, named not for fistfighting but after the Hindi word *panch*, or 'five things', was traditionally made with rum, citrus and at least three spices, often including cinnamon, nutmeg and ginger or cloves. It is in Jamaica that we find the first references to this beverage, which introduced distilled molasses to polite society. Punches made from brandy or whisky with fruit juice and sugar had been recorded as early as the 1630s, but rum punches quickly became popular wherever the raw materials were available.

Rum punch was standardized in 1694 in a set of regulations that the English issued in Bombay, which specified: 'if any man comes into a victualling house to drink punch, he may demand one quart good Goa arak, half a pound of sugar, and half a pint of good lime water, and make his own punch.' This beverage, called Bombay Government Punch, lacks the expensive spices that add aroma and complexity, but could be made cheaply, and like grog was a healthier beverage than straight rum. (It packs a wallop; if you decide to make one using this recipe, it is best to add water or tea.)

Morewood records a similar drink on St Kitts called a 'swizzle' in 1838, which he referred to as

> rum with about six times the quantity of water, rendered palatable by the infusion of some aromatic ingredients. This beverage is often expensive, because water has frequently to be brought in from the neighboring islands, and sometimes rum and wine is given in exchange.

The fact that the water was more expensive than the rum in this era is mind-boggling to a modern person eyeing the prices for good rum at liquor stores. The splinter of wood that was used to spear fruit in this drink, the swizzle stick, was more than just decoration, since it was made from an aromatic wood that added a slight root beer flavour.

There was a craze for rum punch in England beginning in the 1720s, and punch houses opened all over the country. The most elegant establishments charged exorbitant prices: in 1730 a bowl of the best punch could sell for eight shillings a quart, at a time when a week's room and board in London was only seven shillings. The popularity of punch continued through the Regency era, and exotic versions flavoured with expensive spices were served at royal events. It was popular on the other side of the Atlantic too, and the recipe for the rum punch that Martha Washington served to guests is included in the section at the end of this book.

Punch declined in popularity in Britain, but new versions flourished in the Caribbean. The Myers's Rum company claims that the first Planter's Punch was served at the opening of their distillery in 1893, but the first known reference in print to Planter's Punch was this poetic recipe in the 8 August 1908 edition of the *New York Times*:

This recipe I give to thee,
Dear brother in the heat.
Take two of sour (lime let it be)
To one and a half of sweet,
Of Old Jamaica pour three strong,
And add four parts of weak.
Then mix and drink. I do no wrong –
I know whereof I speak.

Myers's version of Planter's Punch includes orange juice and a dash of grenadine, and is a much more sophisticated drink. Punches have remained popular for good reason: they're enormously refreshing, and the juice and spices can conceal the imperfections of even mediocre liquor.

The period of French and Spanish colonialism on the mainland led to the creation of a rum drink that is no longer associated with rum. In Stanley Arthur Clisby's book, *Famous New Orleans Drinks and How to Mix 'Em* (1937), he provides a recipe for a rum mint julep, calling it the original mint julep that arrived in Louisiana in 1793 when white aristocrats who were expelled from Santo Domingo settled in New Orleans. The earliest known mention of a mint julep, from 1803, only calls it a 'spiritous liquor with mint in it', so it is quite likely that whiskey was not used in the first versions.

Other rum drinks were being created in South America at about the same time, but unfortunately with much less documentation. Brazil and Mexico both lay claim to very different drinks called *rompope*. The Mexican version is a sweet vanilla-infused eggnog, which was reportedly invented in a convent in Puebla in the late 1600s. In Brazil this is rum with

Rum punch was the tipple of choice for upper-class Englishmen in the 1700s. It was not always drunk in moderation, as shown in *A Midnight Modern Conversation,* William Hogarth's wonderful depiction of a drunken rum punch party, 1732.

cinnamon, sugar and bitter lemon, with a sister drink called *dimantina* that is the same with milk added.

While we have at least a vague timeline for these drinks, it is impossible to accurately date one of the most interesting rum beverages. The *Quarente Quatre* or '44' is peculiar to Madagascar, and involves cutting 44 slits into an orange, filling each slit with a coffee bean, and putting the orange into a jar containing a litre of white rum for 44 days. This obviously isn't something you'd whip up on short notice, but it is an amazing drink. If you don't like coffee you can make it with cloves for a spicy, citrusy cordial.

Cooling drinks were deservedly popular in India and in the New World's steamy summers, but just as important were the eggnogs and hot toddies that warmed up winter evenings. The hot drink known as flip, described in an earlier chapter, also appears in a poem from 1704 that mentions bounce, cherries soaked in rum:

> The days are short, the weather's cold
> By tavern fires tales are told
> Some ask for dram when first come in
> Others with flip and bounce begin.

A hot rum drink that is enduringly popular is Austrian *jagertee*, which at its simplest is just rum poured into tea. A drink by that name, which means 'hunter's tea' in German, was invented in the nineteenth century, but it isn't known whether it contained the herbs that give the modern bottled version its distinctive flavour. It doesn't help that the drink was known under various other names such as hut tea, ranger's tea and poacher's tea, supposedly depending on the percentage of alcohol. A recipe for 'Oberjagertee', or chief-hunter tea, has twice the amount of alcohol, and 'Schürzenjagertee', hunting-something-in-a-skirt tea, contains three times the amount. One suspects that anyone who drinks this is really hunting for oblivion, and would soon find it.

Eggnog has been a traditional drink for centuries, and there are many elaborate recipes from colonial America onwards. One of the most enjoyable that I have tried is relatively modern; it is called Moose Milk and is a favourite drink of the Canadian Air Force at their New Year's celebrations. As a glance at the recipe at the back of the book shows, milking a moose is not required to make the drink.

I could easily go on with twentieth-century rum drinks from the tiki era like the Zombie, Mai Tai and the lethal Missionary's Downfall, but don't see a point in doing so in this book. Bartending historian Jeff 'Beachbum' Berry has written a definitive and entertaining work on the subject, and I can do no better than to point you toward that book on the Suggested Reading list.

The History of Cooking with Rum

Like many alcoholic drinks, rum changes its character remarkably when cooked, but it also can be used uncooked to enhance other flavours. It is popular as a filling for chocolates, and can be used to soak fruitcakes and rum babas. It can be used to produce a wonderfully delicate and aromatic cake, and it has served as the base for barbecue, Jamaican jerk and other savoury sauces.

There are many recipes from colonial America that use rum, most often in sweet dishes such as apple tansy tarts, baked apples with rum raisins and rum berry sauces. An excellent modern interpretation of one of these is the strawberry rum sauce served over a Dutch Baby pancake – see the

It has been claimed that the rum cake evolved from a steamed pudding popular in the 17th century. This cake was made using the recipe from Mr Cecil's Restaurant.

recipe section for details of these and other items from this chapter.

Another old combination that is difficult to date is rum butter, which was certainly drunk as hot buttered rum as early as the colonial era, but wasn't documented in cooking until much later. The oldest specific citation I've found is from 1889, and it didn't make the *Oxford English Dictionary* until 1939, but it's hard to believe it really was invented that recently. New Orleans cookbooks from the 1920s refer to rum butter sauces as old family recipes, and rum butter glazes for bread puddings are an old tradition in the city. There are numerous earlier references to 'hard sauce', made with butter and various liquors, but most seem to regard whiskey, brandy and rum as interchangeable.

The first attributed recipe I have found that uses rum is a surprising one – a rum omelette that is associated with Thomas Jefferson. If you're used to savoury omelettes filled with ham or cheese, this egg pancake topped with rum-apricot sauce will be a revelation. America's third president had a well-deserved reputation as a culinary adventurer but was not a hands-on cook; his French chef may have experimented with rum as a substitute for brandy. It was not specified whether this omelette was intended to be a main dish, snack or dessert, but it makes a simple but elegant brunch item.

The item that brought rum to the attention of cooks in Europe was the rum baba, which was first made in Paris in the nineteenth century. King Stanislas of Poland had brought the yeast cakes called *babkas* to France during his exile in the 1720s, and the French hit on the idea of soaking them in brandy. Around 1835 a patisserie in Paris decided to use rum instead, and a star was born. The ring cake mould that is usually used for rum babas was invented in 1844, and in that form the rum baba spread across Europe, with a variant becoming a speciality of Naples. Other rum-soaked cakes followed, and they became a Christmas tradition as far away as Kerala in South India. (Some people have attributed the rum baba to the great French gourmet Brillat-Savarin. A variant on the rum baba was named for him, not by him – he died five years before the first rum baba was recorded, and there is no mention of it in his great book *The Physiology of Taste*.)

Rum balls are another Christmas tradition in which the rum is not baked, so the cake is mildly alcoholic. They seem to have originated around 1850 in Germany, where they are called *Rumkugel*, but there are many regional variations; in one Hungarian version called *kókuszgolyó* the rum and chocolate mix is rolled around a whole cherry, then the rum ball is rolled around coconut flakes.

Sweet rum desserts are not only popular in Europe; there are many fine ones from the New World, such as '*claypot canela*' sauce from Colombia. This mix of rum, cinnamon, sugar and star anise is usually made with *panela*, boiled raw sugar-cane juice, but you can use brown sugar and get an almost identical effect. The caramel-flavoured sauce with a mild rum tang can be used to frost a cake or fill a cream puff, and is the most distinctively Colombian dessert.

Finally, we come to one of the signature items of New Orleans cuisine: Bananas Foster. This was invented in 1950, either by Owen Edward Brennan or Paul Blange, both of whom were chefs at Brennan's Restaurant in the French Quarter. It was named for Richard Foster, the head of the New Orleans Crime Commission, a gourmet who dined at the restaurant regularly. The dessert of bananas flamed with rum, cinnamon and banana liqueur was an immediate hit, and Brennan's now uses 35,000 lb (15,876 kg) of bananas a year making the confection.

Though sweet rum sauces dominate cookbooks, rum has also been used as a base for savoury sauces. Some Jamaican jerk sauces use rum as an ingredient, chilli made with rum has placed well in cookoffs in Texas, and honey-rum sauces have been used to baste chicken and fish in the

Philippines and elsewhere. In the tiki 1950s, rum-based barbecue sauces proliferated, usually in the form of a sweet, sticky coating for spare ribs and other grilled meats. Rum-ginger sauces also date from this era, and though these were often claimed to be traditional Polynesian or Caribbean dishes, they were probably created in California. Rum-based grilling sauces really hit their stride in the 1970s, and there are many rum, ginger and citrus sauces to choose from at any high-end grocery.

There are many other recipes that involve cooking with rum, and a book could easily be written on the topic, but as far as I know no such work exists. It would be an interesting volume that would show the subtle side of a powerful liquor.

The Future of Rum

Rum is finally being treated as seriously as brandy, fine whisky and other liquors, and distillers have responded by coming up with an unprecedented range of flavours and styles. Some of these sound bizarre, such as the aged sorghum-based rum made in Madison, Wisconsin, by Yahara Bay distillers. In blind tastings I conducted among rum lovers, everyone commented on the unusual combination of musky and herbal flavours, but not one suggested that it was anything but rum.

The average quality of rum has certainly risen worldwide, and even countries that once produced famously bad rum are now bottling high-end liquor and selling it at premium prices. The British Admiralty derided rum from Mauritius in the nineteenth century; it is now sold as Starr African Rum and celebrated for its hints of citrus and cardamom. Traditional producers like Appleton's of Jamaica are selling rum that has been aged for as long as 30 years and promoting it at expensive events in which rum is paired with foods in the manner of fine wines. These dinners have been less than successful, since rum is too alcoholic to really work with food pairings the way subtler wines and beers do, but the mere fact that the concept is being tried is a sign of serious intent.

Of course there are rivers of bad rum being made as well, since government price supports make overproduction of sugar a certainty. There have also been whiffs of scandal from some quarters about misrepresentation of the age of rums, and of artificial concoctions added to young rums to make them appear aged. In the same way that many people embrace genetically modified crops and molecular gastronomy, this kind of tinkering may eventually be seen as not merely acceptable but desirable. Purists and those who revere tradition will recoil, but a generation that has grown up drinking spiced and fruited

Occasionally a bottle of extremely old rum is found in someone's cellar and is sold at extraordinary prices. These bottles of Jamaican rum from 1875 have an estimated value of €500 each.

Decent rum is made in some very unlikely places. Old Jamaica is made in Ireland from Caribbean molasses.

rums is liable to be excited by post-cultural experiments that taste like nothing else on earth.

The simultaneous booms in premium traditional rums and fruit- or spice-flavoured versions is likely to continue with both sides upping the ante. Expect to see older and more exotic rums sold at spiralling prices at the same time that hipsters explore using rum in vodka and gin drinks and in ever more outré combinations. The slaves who toiled in the cachaça fields with tafia, sailors who hoisted a tipple before splicing the rigging, and gentlemen with flappers on their arm who frequented speakeasies wouldn't recognize either the refined or the exotically blended beverages, but they're all pages in a story that gets longer every day.

Recipes

Rum Drinks

It is hard to pick recipes from the bartender's manual of history to include here, but it seems best to focus on those that are not in most mixologists' repertoire or easily available elsewhere. Following are a few that are easy to make and only use commonly available ingredients.

Rum Shrub
(1670s)

This hot-weather drink is making a comeback, and though several recipes are available from the colonial era, most are for making amounts suitable for a tavern full of thirsty people. This modern version can be made with any berries, though raspberries were called for in the original.

1 cup (225 ml) water
1 cup (200 g) sugar
4 cups (700 g) raspberries or chopped strawberries
2 cups (450 ml) white wine vinegar (not white vinegar)

Whisk water and sugar together to a boil. Reduce heat and add the raspberries, stirring for 10 minutes. Add the vinegar and boil for 2 minutes. Pour the liquid and push the berries through a strainer, cool, bottle, and let sit for at least a day. The shrub mix will keep in a refrigerator for up to a month. To use, mix shrub 2-to-1-to 1 with rum and water, or for added flavour and fizz, use ginger beer or ginger ale instead of water.

Landlord May's Flip
(1671)

2 lb (900 g) sugar
2 eggs
½ pint (225 ml) cream
dark beer or amber ale
cheap light rum

Mix sugar, eggs, and cream and let stand in the refrigerator or a cool room for two days. To serve, fill a quart mug two-thirds full of beer, add four heaping spoonfuls of the above mixture, then thrust in a hot poker until the mixture bubbles vigorously. Add a gill of rum just before serving, and drink hot. I have used Belgian dark ales and Mexican amber beers with good results. Warning – when the poker is thrust into the cold beer mix, it foams up a lot – only fill the pitcher about two-thirds of the way or it will overflow.

Martha Washington's Rum Punch
(1780)

4 fl. oz. (115 ml) simple syrup (sugar water, see any bar guide)
4 fl. oz. (115 ml) lemon juice
4 fl. oz. (115 ml) fresh orange juice
3 fl. oz. (85 ml) white rum
3 fl. oz. (85 ml) dark rum
3 fl. oz. (85 ml) orange Curaçao
3 lemons, quartered
1 orange, quartered

½ tsp grated nutmeg
3 cinnamon sticks (broken)
6 cloves
12 oz. (340 ml) boiling water

In a container, mash the orange, lemons, cinnamon sticks, cloves and nutmeg. Add the syrup and the lemon and orange juices. Pour the boiling water over the mixture in the container. Let it cool for a few minutes. When cool, add the white rum, dark rum and orange Curacao.

Strain well into a pitcher or punch bowl. Serve over ice in goblets and decorate each glass with wheels of lemon and orange.

Moose Milk
(Twentieth century)

12 large eggs
1 cup (200 g) plus 2 tbsp sugar
4¼ pints (2 litres) vanilla ice cream
4 cups (900 ml) milk
¾ cup (170 ml) dark rum
4 cups (900 ml) light rum or brandy

Separate the eggs. In a large bowl, beat the egg yolks. Beat in half the sugar, a little at a time, and beat the mixture until it is light and lemon-coloured. In another bowl, beat the egg whites until frothy. Beat in the remaining half of the sugar. Continue beating the mixture until it thickens.

In a larger bowl, combine the two mixtures and stir in the milk and rum (or brandy). Chill the Moose Milk, covered overnight. Transfer it to a punch bowl. Cut the ice cream into small pieces and stir into mixture. Let it stand 10 minutes before serving.

Serves 10; if desired, you may sprinkle with cinnamon before serving.

Cooking with Rum

Dutch Baby with Rum Sauce

This Pennsylvania Dutch-style recipe is an adaptation by Laura Flowers, aka The Cooking Photographer. Her cooking blog is an excellent resource.

for the Fresh Strawberry Rum Syrup
½ cup (115 ml) water
½ cup (100 g) granulated sugar
2 cups (350 g) strawberries
zest of 1 lemon
2 tbsp white or dark rum (I use Myers's dark)
small pinch of salt

Clean, hull and purée the strawberries in a food processor. Set aside.

In a medium-sized saucepan over medium high heat boil the water and sugar until clear. Add the puréed strawberries, lemon zest, rum and salt. Bring to a boil and then lower the temperature until the mixture is at a high simmer. Cook for 15 minutes, stirring occasionally. The syrup will thicken more as it cools.

(This makes twice as much syrup as would be used by one Dutch Baby. The leftover syrup will keep for a day or two in the refrigerator and is delicious over ice cream.)

for the Dutch Baby
2 eggs, at room temperature
½ cup (115 ml) milk
¼ teaspoon salt
½ cup (100 g) all purpose flour
3 tbsp unsalted butter
1 cup (175 g) sliced strawberries
powdered (icing) sugar
strawberry rum syrup (recipe above)

Preheat the oven to 220°C (425°F).

Beat together the eggs, milk and salt. Then beat the flour into the mixture until smooth.

In a 9- to 10-inch skillet (20–25-cm frying pan), melt the butter over medium heat on the stovetop. Pour in the mixture and cook for exactly one minute. Place the skillet in the oven and immediately turn the oven down to 175°C (350°F). Bake until puffed over the edges and nicely browned; about 15 minutes.

Remove from the oven and top with the strawberries, sugar and strawberry rum syrup. Slide onto a plate, cut in half, and move half to another plate. Serve immediately.

Serves two very hungry people.

Thomas Jefferson's Rum Omelette

6 eggs, beaten
½ tsp salt
3 tbsp sugar
4 tbsp rum
2 tbsp butter
2 tbsp powdered (icing) sugar
4 tbsp apricot jam (preserves)

Add salt, sugar and half the rum to the beaten eggs. Beat again until fluffy. Heat the butter in an omelette pan, pour in the egg mixture and cook until firm, lifting up from sides. When firm throughout but still a little moist, fold over and slip onto a warm platter. Sprinkle with the powdered sugar. Make a sauce of the remaining rum and preserves. Pour over the omelette and serve immediately.

(President Jefferson had quite a sweet tooth. If you don't, make this without the powdered sugar, or with half the amount called for in the recipe. Pair this with something savoury like sausages or bacon at brunch, or surprise your guests and make it as a dessert.)

Mr Cecil's Rum Cake

While writing this book, I tried several rum cakes. This one, from a family recipe of film director Jonathan Burrows, owner of Mr Cecil's restaurants in California, was by far the best.

1 cup (115 g) finely chopped pecans
3 cups (330 g) cake flour (low-gluten, finely milled flour)]
1 tbsp baking powder
½ tsp salt
1 cup (8 ounces or 230 g) unsalted butter, room temperature
2 cups (454 g) granulated sugar
5 large eggs
¾ cup (10 fl. oz.) buttermilk
1 package french vanilla pudding, or 1 ounce (30 g) custard powder
½ cup (115 ml) light rum
Sauce:
1 stick (110 g) unsalted butter
1 cup (100 g) sugar
¼ cup (55 ml) water
2 fl. oz. (55 ml) rum

Preheat oven to 350°F (175°C). Sprinkle the chopped pecans on the bottom of a greased bundt pan. In a medium bowl, stir together with a wire whisk the flour, baking powder, vanilla pudding mix and salt. Cut up the butter into 1-inch (2.5-cm) pieces and place them in the large bowl of an electric mixer, fitted with a paddle attachment or beaters. Beat for 3 minutes on medium-high speed until the butter is light and creamy in colour. Stop and scrape the bowl. Cream the butter for an additional 60 seconds, then add the sugar, a quarter-cup at a time, beating for one minute after each addition. Scrape the sides of the bowl occasionally. Add the eggs one at a time. Reduce the mixer speed. Stir rum into the buttermilk. Add the dry ingredients alternately with the buttermilk. Mix until just incorporated. Scrape the sides of the bowl and mix for 15 seconds longer.

Spoon the batter into the prepared pan. Lift up the pan with the batter, and let it drop onto the counter top to burst any air bubbles, allowing the batter to settle, then put in the oven. Rotate the pan after 30 minutes and check every 5–10 minutes after cake has baked for 1 hour. The cake is done when a toothpick inserted into the cake's centre comes out clean. When the cake is almost done, bring the sauce to a boil, stir and remove from the heat. Pour the sauce over the cake and let it cool completely (approximately 1 hour), then remove from the pan.

Select Bibliography

Berry, Jeff, *Sippin' Safari: In Search of the Great Lost Tropical Drink Recipes and the People Behind Them* (San Jose, CA, 2007)
This history of the rise and fall of Polynesian bar craze is a humorous and enjoyable read and recommended to anyone with an interest in the subject. It contains plenty of recipes for the favourites and some obscure tipples, and is a practical bartending guide to recreating these drinks.

Curtis, Wayne, *. . . And a Bottle of Rum* (New York, 2007)
Covers the history of the Caribbean rum trade in great depth, but later developments in a more cursory manner.

Earle, Alice Morse, *Customs and Fashions in Old New England*
An excellent survey of society of the 1700s, with chapters focusing on food and drink. It is available online through The Gutenberg Project.

Gjelten, Tom, *Bacardi and the Long Fight For Cuba* (New York, 2008)
The surprisingly interesting history of the Bacardi family. Gjelten profiles several generations of talented and ruthless businessmen who made rum and money in a horribly misgoverned county, and this history reads at times like a political thriller.

Morewood, Samuel, *A Philosophical and Statistical History of the Inventions and Customs of Ancient and Modern Nations in the*

Manufacture and Use of Inebriating Liquors (London, 1838). Samuel Morewood was an exciseman, but his interest in alcohol extended far beyond collecting taxes on the liquor that flowed through the British Empire. His exhaustive history of the arts of fermenting and distilling ran over 700 pages and includes fantastically arcane lore, but is briskly written so a modern reader may enjoy it. Several editions are available for free online; I used the one at Archive.org.

Williams, Ian, *Rum, a Social and Sociable History* (New York, 2005)
Also covers the history of the Caribbean rum trade, with less on more recent history

Wondrich, David, *Punch: Delights and Dangers of the Flowing Bowl* (New York, 2010)
A gifted writer explores the history of punch in a way that is always insightful and often hilarious. This book includes many period recipes, including Charles Dickens's own recipe for rum punch.

Websites and Associations

Peter's Rum Pages

www.rum.cz

The labels from rum bottles often feature beautiful art, and Peter's Rum Pages has the definitive online collection of rum labels through history. It is sorted by country or company, and often has historical information about rum production. The site is headquartered in the Czech Republic but is maintained in good English.

AMountainOfCrushedIce.com

One of the more interesting websites about the history and technique of bartending, and there are many articles about rum drinks.

MinistryOfRum.com

An excellent source for rum reviews and a good place to get rum questions answered.

rumhistory.com

A compendium of rum lore, songs, and cultural references. This site was created by the author, and has some interesting additional material that I did not have room for in this book. If you'd like to hear the sea shanties that are quoted here or know more about the culture of rum, this is the place to go.

rumandcocacolareader.com

A page all about the true history behind the famous song, which is far more complex than generally recognized.

rumproject.com

Captain Jimbo's Rum Project is a site with much to say about rum, some of it controversial but all of it entertainingly written.

Rum Museums

There are many small museums of rum production located in distilleries around the world, though some of these are more glorified gift shops than serious institutions. These inevitably focus on the brand of rum produced there, but some, including the Havana Club Museum in Cuba and the St James Museum in Martinique, are reported to have good general interest exhibits.

Among the museums not affiliated with any particular distillery are the following:

Dominican Republic
Rum and Sugar Cane Museum,
Isabel La Catolica #261,
Santo Domingo.

This museum is located in a sixteenth-century building in the tourist zone, and has a bar with sampling offered.

Germany
Das Rum-Museum
Located inside the Seafaring Museum,
Schiffbrucke 39, 24939 Flensburg.

This is a small museum in the basement of a former rum warehouse. www.flensburg-online.de/museum/rum-museum.html

Great Britain
The Rum Story,
Lowther Street, Whitehaven, Cumbria

Located in a set of rum warehouses dating to 1785, this museum includes exhibits on production, smuggling, a reconstructed boiling room and distillery, and so on.
www.rumstory.co.uk.

Martinique
Musée de la Canne,
Point Vatable, Trois-Islets.

Though the St James distillery museum is larger and more famous, this little museum is worth a visit if you are on the island.

Acknowledgements

I am indebted to many people for their assistance with this book, and can't name them all because I am already so far over my agreed-upon word count that my editor will be cutting this manuscript with a machete. I must thank the following major contributors: nautical historian Simon Spalding for help with maritime lore, American colonial history and sea shanties; Voodoo scholar Gerry Gandolfo; Charles Perry for odd details and general encouragement; Joe and Gail Touch for assistance with Portuguese translations and rum lore; Chulatip Nitibhon for help resolving Southeast Asian rum history; Marshall Sheetz of the Colonial Williamsburg Foundation and Steve Bashore, Manager of the Gristmill and Distillery at Mount Vernon, for their expertise on measurements; editor Andy Smith for patience and guidance; Wolf Foss for drinking any concoction I made and honestly critiquing the result, and my beloved wife Jace Foss for putting up with over a year of rum drinks and strange kitchen experiments.

To all the rest of you who helped me refine this, tasted arcane recipes and generally encouraged me, my deepest thanks. Any errors in this manuscript are my own fault, because I had wonderful and willing help.

Photo Acknowledgements

The author and the publishers wish to express their thanks to the below sources of illustrative material and/or permission to reproduce it:

Phoebe Beach, used by permission, with thanks to Mutual Publishing: p. 95; Biodiversity Heritage Library: p. 26; British Library, London: pp. 22, 25, 28, 43, 81; © The Trustees of the British Museum, London: p. 44; David Croy's Advertising Archive: p. 51; www.finestandrarest.com, used by permission: pp. 47, 73, 96; photo by Richard Foss: pp. 72, 79, 110, 118, 123; Photo by W. L. Foss: p. 34; FotoLibra: p. 84 (Martin Hendry); Courtesy of Galleries L'Affichiste, Montreal: p. 82; Grindon Collection, Manchester Museum Herbarium: pp. 11, 21; Istockphoto: p. 6 (Jaime Villalta); Cachaça Leblon: p. 76; Library of Congress, Washington, DC: pp. 12, 16, 49, 55, 78, 90; US National Library of Medicine, Bethesda, Maryland: p. 17; Princeton University Library: p. 88; Proximo Spirits, used by permission: pp. 93, 100, 102, 122; Rex Features: p. 103 (Isifa Image Service sro); Starr African Rum: p. 107; State Library of New South Wales: p. 68; State Library of Queensland: pp. 69, 71; Victoria and Albert Museum, London: p. 23; Vintage Scans Creative Commons: p. 8; Werner Forman Archive: p. 7 (Formerly Philip Goldman Collection. Location 17).

Index

italic numbers refer to illustrations; **bold** to recipes